Levi David Addai

House of Agnes

Methuen Drama

Published by Methuen Drama 2008

1 3 5 7 9 10 8 6 4 2

Methuen Drama
A & C Black Publishers Limited
38 Soho Square
London W1D 3HB
www.acblack.com

ISBN 978 1 408 10834 5

A CIP catalogue record for this book
is available from the British Library

Typeset by Country Setting, Kingsdown, Kent

Acknowledgements

I'd like to thank God, Seleena Lewis, *the man-dem* – Agyeman Lewis, Warren G and Manny O., Stacey Lewis, Richy D. – and my mum. Love you all.

I'd like to give heartfelt thanks to Roxana Silbert, Pippa Ellis, Ushi Bagga and George Perrin for seeing the potential of the play from the early stages and their encouragement throughout. Thank you, thank you, thank you, thank you!

I'd also like to thank Howard Gooding, Dawn Walton and the Peggy Ramsay Foundation for their generous support, much appreciated.

From small ideas do great decisions grow . . .

Paines Plough
in association with
Oval House Theatre
presents

House of Agnes

by Levi David Addai

First performed at Oval House Theatre on 6 March 2008

Cast *in order of appearance*

Agnes Ofori	**Cecilia Noble**
Caleb Mensah	**Anwar Lynch**
Solomon Mensah	**Ludvig Bonin**
Davina Marshall	**Sheri-An Davis**
Mehmet Sas	**Adam Deacon**
Michaela Boyd	**Catherine Bailey**
Director	**George Perrin**
Designer	**Hannah Clark**
Lighting Designer	**Chahine Yavroyan**
Production Manager	**Robert Holmes**
Stage Manager	**Jemma Gardner**
Sound Technician	**Giles Thomas**
Design Assistant	**Poppy Lozynski**
Press Representative	**Sheridan Humphreys** (07966 578607)
Cover Image	**iStockphoto.com/ Chris Schmidt**

House of Agnes is a Paines Plough Commission.

The play-script that follows was correct at the time of going to press but may have changed during rehearsal.

Paines Plough and Oval House Theatre would like to thank: Christabel Anderson, Amy Ball, Paul Handley, Nick Lidster, Ellen McDougall, Indhu Rubasingham, David Salter, Gary Thorne, Ché Walker, Sasha Wares.

The Company

Levi David Addai | Writer

Levi's first play, *93.2FM* was performed at the Royal Court Theatre in 2005 and then revived in 2006 before touring to Cardiff, Birmingham, Liverpool and Brighton. A pilot script based on *93.2FM* has been commissioned by BBC TV.

House of Agnes was written as part of an attachment at Paines Plough in February 2007 and was subsequently commissioned and developed with the company.

A reading of Levi's second play *Oxford Street* took place at the Soho Theatre in April 2007 as part of Tiata Fahodzi's 10th Birthday Festival. *Oxford Street* will be produced at the Royal Court Theatre in May 2008.

Levi was a member of Soho Theatre's Core Group Writers Programme in 2005/6 and completed an attachment at the Royal Court Theatre in Spring 2007. In 2006 Levi was chosen as one of 'The Fifty' – a group of writers selected to take part in a series of workshops and seminars organised by the BBC writersroom as part of the Royal Court's 50th birthday celebrations.

Catherine Bailey | Michaela Boyd

Catherine trained at the Italia Conti Academy of Theatre Arts and Guildhall School of Music and Drama.

Recent theatre credits include: *The Country Wife* (Theatre Royal Haymarket), *Sit and Shiver* (New End Theatre and Hackney Empire), *Walk Hard - Talk Loud* (Tricycle Theatre), *The Life and Times of Young Bob Scallion* (Northcott Theatre), *Newsrevue* (Canal Cafe), *Headstate* (Landor Theatre), *'Tis Pity She's a Whore* (Young Vic) and *Spring Awakening* (Royal Shakespeare Company).

Television credits include: *EastEnders* (BBC), *The Bill* (ITV), *The English Harem* (Feelgood Fiction), *Egypt* (BBC), *Rosemary and Thyme* (Carnival Productions), *55 Degrees North* (BBC), *My Family* (BBC), *High Stakes* (LWT), *Urban Gothic* (Channel Five), *The Infinite Worlds of H.G. Wells* (Hallmark Productions), *Residents* (BBC), *Hawk* (BBC), *Peak Practice* (Central), *Holby City* (BBC) and *The Wild House* (BBC).

Film credits include: *The Grind* (Dangerous Films), *It's Not You It's Me* (Hopscotch Films) and *Beginner's Luck* (Angel Film and Television).

She is also a member of The Factory Theatre Company, who regularly perform *Hamlet* at various locations across London (Riverside Studios, Southwark Playhouse, Pacific Playhouse, The Pleasance and Wilton's Music Hall).

Ludvig Bonin | Solomon Mensah

Ludvig trained at The Academy of Live and Recorded Arts.

Recent theatre credits include: *Fit* (UK Tour), *Stonewall* (Drill Hall & Pleasance Theatre), *Ask and Tell* (Tristan Bates Theatre), *Trumpet* (Drill Hall), *Taken In* (Tristan Bates Theatre), *Totally Practically Naked In My Room On A Wednesday Night* (Tristan Bates Theatre), *Bashment* (Theatre Royal Stratford East), *Laters* (Tristan Bates Theatre) and *Sweet Love Adieu* (Bowen West Theatre).

Television and Film credits include: *EastEnders* (BBC), *Souljah* (B3 Productions), *Batch* (Complete Works Ltd), *The Checklist* (Yolo inc/Milkshake) and *Fools Circle* (Tin Can Productions).

Sheri-An Davis | Davina Marshall

Sheri-An trained at Central School of Speech and Drama.

Recent theatre credits include: *Torn* (Arcola Theatre), *Brixton Stories* (Lyric Hammersmith), *Basin Street Blues* (Jermyn Street Theatre) and *As You Like It, The Crucible* and *Twelfth Night* (Central School).

Television credits include: *My Family* (BBC), *After You've Gone* (BBC). Her latest film credit is *Spoil* (Channel Four).

Adam Deacon | Mehmet Sas

Adam trained at The Anna Sher Theatre.

Recent theatre credits include: *East is East* (Pilot Theatre), *Playing Fields* (Soho Theatre), *Go Lem Go* (Pop Up Theatre), *Dr Sues* (Old Vic), *Oliver* (London Palladium) and a range of T.I.E work with the Y Touring Theatre Company.

Television credits include: *The Bill* (ITV), *Casualty* (BBC), *A Touch of Frost* (ITV), *London's Burning* (LWT), *Spooks* (BBC), *Wall of Silence* (ITV), *Is Harry On The Boat* (SKY1), *Passer By* (BBC), *The Coral Island* (ITV), *English Express* (BBC), *Teenage Sexuality* (Channel Four), *Goodness Gracious Me* (BBC), *Bills New Frock* (Channel Four), *Eastenders* (BBC), *Love Soup* (BBC), *Gunrush* (ITV), *West 10 LDN* (BBC3), *Sugar Rush* (Channel Four) and *Dubplate Drama* (Channel Four).

Film credits include: *Kidulthood* (Stealth Films), *Ali G In Da House* (Working Title), *Wilderness* (Ecosse Films) and *Sugarhouse* (Collision Ltd). Adam has just finished filming *Adulthood*, the sequel to *Kidulthood*.

Cecilia Noble | Agnes Ofori

Cecilia trained at Central School of Speech and Drama.

Recent theatre credits include: *The Exonnerated* (Riverside/Dublin), *Yellowman* (Hampstead Theatre), *His Dark Materials, Henry V* and *The Recruiting Officer* (National Theatre), *A Raisin In The Sun* (Young Vic), *Wine In The Wilderness, Water, Pecong, The Piano Lesson, Playboy of the West Indies* and *Iced* (Tricycle), *The Tempest* (Cheek By Jowl), *Mill Fire* (Bush Theatre), *The Birthday Party* (Shared Experience), *Young Writers Festival, Talking in Tongues, This Is A Chair* and *The Sacred Heart* (Royal Court Theatre), *Blues For Mister Charlie* (Royal Exchange Theatre), *The Rover* (Jacob Film Studio), *Time And The Room* (Nottingham Playhouse), *Amen Corner* (Bristol Old Vic) and *The Vagina Monologues* (Arts Theatre).

Television credits include: 9 episodes of *The Bill* (ITV), *Silent Witness* and *Holby City* (BBC), *Storm Damage* (BBC), *Thieftakers* (Carlton), *Resnick* (BBC), *Casualty* (BBC), *The Rover* (BBC) and *Space Precinct* (Space Productions).

Film credits include: *New Years Day* (New Years Day Ltd), *Native* (Saramar Films Ltd.) and *Mrs Caldicott's Cabbage War* (Cabbage Films).

Anwar Lynch | Caleb Mensah

Anwar trained at the London Academy of Radio, Film & TV and at the Actors Studio, Pinewood Studios.

Recent theatre credits include: *Safe* (West Yorkshire Playhouse), *Billy Liar* and *Our Country's Good* (Arcola Theatre), *Them & Us* (Big Fish Theatre Company), *Bully Beef* (Hackney Empire -Rehearsed Reading), *Out of the Fog* (Almeida Theatre -Workshop) and *The Struggle According to Offor* (Soho Theatre - Rehearsed Reading).

Television credits include: *Sleepless Nights* (The Community Channel).

Film Credits include: *3 Minute Moments* (All Enquiries), *Batch* (Southwark Gangs Film) *Irina P* and *Much Ado About A Minor Ting* (La Famiglia).

Hannah Clark | Designer

Hannah trained in Theatre Design at Nottingham Trent University and in 2005, completed an MA in Scenography with distinction at Central School of Speech and Drama for which she won an A.H.R.C. Award. She was a winner of the 2005 Linbury Biennial Prize for stage design.

Theatre designs include: *The Cracks In My Skin* (Manchester Royal Exchange Studio), *Breakfast With Mugabe* (Theatre Royal Bath), *Ingrid Laubrock Part 1* (Requardt & Company, Centro Coreográfico de Montemor-o-Novo, Portugal), *Othello* (Salisbury Playhouse), *We That Are Left* (Watford Palace Theatre), *Who's Afraid Of Virginia Woolf?* (Royal Exchange Theatre, Manchester), *Big Love* (Gate Theatre), *Terre Haute* (Assembly Rooms, Edinburgh Festival Fringe, Trafalgar Studio 2, UK Tour*)*, *Jammy Dodgers* (Requardt & Company, The Place, Royal Opera House 2, Clore Studio, International Tour), *The Taming Of The Shrew* (Bristol Old Vic), *Death Of A Salesman, What The Butler Saw, Blue/Orange, A View From The Bridge, I Just Stopped By To See The Man, Two* and *Frankie And Johnny In The Clair De Lune* (Octagon Bolton).

Her forthcoming work includes: *As You Like It* (Watford Palace Theatre) and *Ingrid Laubrock Part 2* (Requardt & Company, Teatro Fondamenta Nuove, Venice, The Place).

Jemma Gardner | Stage Manager

Jemma trained at the Royal Academy of Dramatic Art in Stage Management and Technical Theatre. She has also recently completed a contract as Event Co-ordinator (Supply Chain / Site Build) for the 21st World Scout Jamboree. She has worked as Staff Stage Manager for RADA and as the Prop Supervisor for Grange Park Opera season.

Theatre credits include: *Fingerprint* (The Shout), *Blasted* (Graeae Theatre Company), *Billy Liar* (Liverpool Playhouse), *Only Available in Carlisle* (Theatre by the Lake), *Fewer Emergencies* (Royal Court), *The Death of Gogol* and *The 1969 Eurovision Song Contest* (Drill Hall), *World of WearableArt* (WOW, New Zealand), *Elisir d'Amore* (New Zealand Opera), *God's Liar* (Almeida Opera), *Revelations* (Tara Arts), *Tall Stories* (The Shout), *The Butcher's Skin* (Yellow Earth Theatre Company), and *Hamlet* (National Theatre).

Robert Holmes | Production Manager

Robert was the Resident Production Manager at the Bush Theatre 2005– 2008 and Assistant Production Manager at York Theatre Royal 2002-2004.

Productions for the Bush include: *After The End* (Paines Plough), *Bottle Universe, When You Cure Me, Monsieur Ibrahim & The Flowers of the Qur'an, Christmas Is Miles Away, Trad, Crooked, Cruising* (Recorded Delivery), *Pumpgirl, Bones* (Mama Quillo), *I Like Mine With A Kiss, Elling, Tom Fool* (Citizen's Theatre Glasgow), *Trance, How To Curse* and *The Dysfunkshonalz.*

Other production credits include: *Whipping it Up* (New Ambassadors Theatre London & UK National Tour), Stanley Hall Opera 2007, *East* (Leicester Haymarket), *Divine* (Leicester Haymarket) and *Jack & The Beanstalk* (Newbury Corn Exchange).

His forthcoming work includes: Longborough Festival Opera for Summer 2008.

George Perrin | Director

George trained as assistant and associate director to Roxana Silbert at Paines Plough on *Long Time Dead* (Drum and Traverse) and *After The End* (Bush, Traverse, UK and International Tour); in receipt of the Genesis Director's Award at the Young Vic; and on the National Theatre Studio Director's Course.

For Paines Plough George has directed *The Dirt Under the Carpet* and *Crazy Love* at the Shunt Vaults, *My Little Heart Dropped in Coffee* and *Babies* for Wild Lunch at the Young Vic; and co-directed *Murder at Gobbler's Wood* at the Latitude Festival.

George is co-founder and Artistic Director of nabokov for whom he has directed *Terre Haute* (Assembly Rooms Edinburgh, Trafalgar Studio 2, UK Tour) and *Camarilla* (Old Red Lion, Edinburgh Festival Fringe).

George is currently Trainee Associate Director of Paines Plough and Watford Palace Theatre.

Chahine Yavroyan | Lighting Designer

Chahine trained at the Bristol Old Vic Theatre School.

Recent theatre work includes: *Long Time Dead, Strawberries in January* and *After the End* (Paines Plough), *Damascus* and *When the Bulbul Stopped Singing* (Traverse), *The Wonderful World of Dissocia, Realism, Elizabeth Gordon Quinn* and *San Diego* (National Theatre of Scotland), *Mahabharata* (Sadler's Wells), *God in Ruins* (Royal Shakespeare Company), *Il Tempo del Postino* (Manchester International Festival), *There's Only One Waine Matthews* (Polka Theatre), *Ornamental Happiness* (Rose English), *How to Live* (Barbican Theatre) and *Othello* (Nottingham Playhouse).

Recent dance work includes: Jasmin Vardimon, Candoco, Frauke Requardt Dance, Bock & Vincenzi, Ricochet, Arthur Pita's Open Heart, Hofesh Schechter, Yolande Snaith Theatredance.

Site-specific work includes: *Enchanted Parks, Dreams of a Winter Night, Deep End* and *Spa* for Geraldine Pilgrim and *Light Touch* (Scarabeus).

Other work includes *Plague Songs* at the Barbican Hall, *The Death of Klinghoffer* for EIF and The Jocelyn Pook Ensemble.

Giles Thomas | Sound Technician

Giles is training at Hurtwood House School, near Guildford, which is a sixth form college that specialises in performing arts. He hopes to continue his training at the Liverpool Institute of Performing Arts where he has been offered a place on their sound technology (BA Hons) course.

House of Agnes by Levi David Addai is kindly supported by Unity Theatre Trust

For the development of the play Paines Plough would like to thank: Richie Campbell, Claire-Louise Cordwell, Lenora Crichlow, Adam Deacon, Abdul Salis and Ellen Thomas.

Paines Plough is an award-winning, nationally and internationally renowned theatre company, specialising exclusively in commissioning and producing new plays.

painesPLOUGH

"The ever-inventive Paines Plough."
The Independent

Inspired by the creativity of our writers and collaborators we've embraced the challenge of diversifying the way in which we work. Our national footprint is far-reaching; our work has recently been seen late at night in the depths of London's West End; over lunch on the South Bank; in St. Petersburg and Bradford, New York and Plymouth; on the Globe Stage and in a cupboard in Brighton.

We seek out partners with whom we can collaborate in a bold, responsive spirit to generate inspiring work. Paines Plough is thrilled to be working with Oval House Theatre to bring this exciting new commission into production.

Paines Plough are:

Artistic Director	Roxana Silbert
General Manager	Ushi Bagga
Literary Manager	Pippa Ellis
Trainee Associate Director	George Perrin
	(supported by Arts Council England)
Interim Administrative Assistant	Fiona Gregory
Playwright in Residence*	Tom Morton-Smith
	(supported by The Fenton Arts Trust and Arts Council England)
Press Representation*	Sheridan Humphries (07966 578607)

Board of Directors: Ola Animashawun, Tamara Cizeika, Giles Croft, David Edwards, Chris Elwell, Fraser Grant, Marilyn Imrie, Clare O'Brien, Jenny Sealey

*Part-time staff

To find out more and join our mailing list visit
www.painesplough.com

Paines Plough is supported by the Arts Council England

Paines Plough is a Registered Charity No 26752

Oval House Theatre is proud to support

Paines Plough in this production of *House of Agnes*.

Oval House Theatre supports and programmes work by some of the most innovative, cutting edge theatre practitioners in Britain and beyond. Working alongside the visiting artists, we offer our expertise and resources to help make good work great.

We are committed to presenting theatre which is relevant to cosmopolitan London, here and now, in all its glory, complexity and challenge.

For more information about Oval House Theatre, our forthcoming season, how to support the work we do, or how to develop your own projects, please see our website www.ovalhouse.com

---

Coming Next From Paines Plough

Paines Plough are joining forces with the Gate Theatre, the National Theatre, Out of Joint and the Royal Court Theatre to present Mark Ravenhill's SHOOT/GET TREASURE/REPEAT, an epic cycle of plays exploring the personal and political effect of war on modern life. Throughout April, the plays will be presented in venues across London, from Sloane Square and the South Bank to a restored Victorian warehouse in Shoreditch.

Paines Plough will capture the spirit of Ravenhill's exquisite mini-masterpieces in the back streets of Shoreditch at the atmospheric Village Underground. Roxana Silbert will direct an extraordinary ensemble of actors in promenade style, offering a cultural catalyst for your East End weekend. Performances will take place from Friday 18 April to Sunday 20 April. Each performance will last approximately an hour and consists of a group of plays.

For more information please visit:
www.shootgettreasurerepeat.com

Paines Plough Residency at Oval House

During the production of *House of Agnes*, Paines Plough will be in residence at Oval House Theatre creating and presenting new work.

Tuesday Night With Levi David Addai
new work at night time

Tuesday 11 March 10.00pm
£5 (£3 *when booked at the same time as House of Agnes*)

Hosted by playwright Levi David Addai, Paines Plough kick off their residency with an evening of brand new work. An eclectic midweek mix-up of evening entertainment.

Tuesday 18 March 10.00pm
£5 (£3 *when booked at the same time as House of Agnes*)

The boldest new talent sought out and commissioned by Levi David Addai to write and perform their own work: a rare late night opportunity to see playwrights on stage.

Why do the British love West African playwrights?

Wednesday 12 March 9.45pm

Join us after the evening performance of *House of Agnes* for a crackling debate about West African playwriting with a panel including Levi David Addai, Dipo Agboluaje and Femi Elufowoju Jr.

House of Agnes – Easter Meal Special

Friday 21 March and Saturday 22 March

Buy a full price ticket to *House of Agnes* and get a play, a meal and a drink all for £12.

For more information please visit www.ovalhouse.com or call the Box Office 020 7582 7680.

House of Agnes

Characters

Agnes Ofori, *mother of Sol and Caleb, black Ghanaian, sixty*
Solomon (Sol) Mensah, *black, twenty-six*
Caleb Mensah, *black, twenty-two*
Davina Marshall, *Sol's girlfriend, black, twenty-four*
Mehmet Sas, *Sol's friend, Turkish, twenty-five*
Michaela Boyd, *white, twenty-nine*

Settings

South-east London, summertime.

Agnes's living room, parks near Caleb's workplace, a park near Agnes's house and Mehmet's uncle's chip shop.

(/) indicates overlapping speech.

Italicised speech indicates characters speaking in their native tongue or slang.

Scene One

The living room of **Agnes**'*s house. A three-seater sofa and a coffee table are in the middle of the room, on top of a large, pearl-white woolen rug. The front door leads into the living room. There is a pile of shoes next to the door. Stairs at the rear of the room lead to the upstairs bedroom. To the left is an entrance to the kitchen.*

Four weeks are left until **Agnes** *leaves the UK.*

Evening. **Caleb** *is doing the final reps of press-ups. He sits on the sofa, out of breath and sweaty. He uses a towel to wipe his face. He puts a finger on his wrist and looks at his watch, as he counts his pulse.*

Agnes *calls from the kitchen.*

Agnes's Voice   CALEB?

Beat.

CALEB?

Caleb   Hmm?

Beat.

Agnes's Voice   CALEB?

Caleb (*sighs*)   What?

Agnes's Voice   Don't 'what' me! (*Kisses her teeth.*)

Beat.

CALEB?

Caleb (*sighs*)   Yes?

Agnes's Voice   Are you hearing me?

Caleb   YES?

Agnes's Voice   Don't say 'Yes', it's 'Yes, Mum'!

Caleb *sighs. Beat.*

Agnes's Voice   CALEB?

Caleb   YES, MUM?

Agnes's Voice   Have you hoovered the living room?

Caleb   Yes.

Beat.

Agnes's Voice   I said, have you hoovered the living / room?

Caleb   YES! I said YES!

Agnes's Voice   Don't say 'Yes', it's 'Yes, Mum'!

Caleb   YES, MUM!

Beat.

Agnes's Voice   Did you hoover the kitchen?

Caleb   Yes, Mum.

Beat.

Agnes's Voice   What about the bedrooms?

Caleb   Yes, Mum.

Beat.

Agnes's Voice   What about the corridor?

Caleb   Yes, Mum, I've hoovered everywhere.

Beat.

Agnes's Voice   Are you sure?

Caleb (*sighs*)   Yes, Mum.

Beat.

Agnes's Voice   It's important you keep the house tidy at all times!

Using the sofa to tuck his feet under, **Caleb** *begins to do some sit-ups on the rug.*

Caleb   Yes, Mum.

Agnes's Voice   It's not when you hear a knock at the door that you begin to tidy your home. Every day you should make sure your house is in order.

Caleb   Yes, Mum.

Beat.

Agnes's Voice   Your clothes are still in the wash basket.

Caleb   I know.

Agnes's Voice   I said your clothes are still / in the wash . . .

Caleb   I said I know!

Agnes's Voice   Your clothes are spilling over.

Caleb   I know.

Agnes's Voice   You need to put them in the washing machine.

Caleb   I know already! I'm trying to concentrate.

Agnes's Voice   What are you up to?

Caleb   Don't worry.

Agnes's Voice   I said what are you up to?

Caleb   Nothing, don't worry!

The doorbell rings.

Agnes's Voice   Go answer the door.

Caleb   Are you expecting anyone?

Agnes's Voice   Just go and answer the door!

Caleb   All right!

He gets up and answers the door. **Sol** *and* **Davina** *enter, holding hands.*

Caleb   Oh, it's you.

Sol   Problem?

Caleb   Na, na. Just when you come to my house unannounced . . .

Sol   This ain't your house you fool, come out the way.

Caleb   Fool? Moi?

Agnes's Voice   Caleb, who's at the door?

Caleb   Jehovah Witness.

Sol *hits his brother.*

Caleb   Oww!

Davina (*to* **Sol**)   Oi!

Sol (*to* **Davina**)   What? (*Shouts towards kitchen.*) It's me, Mum!

Agnes's Voice   Okay, I'm coming.

Davina (*to* **Sol**)   Are you sure she's going to listen?

Sol   There's no way she'd leave with this still going on. Everything will be all right, babes, trust. (*To* **Caleb**.) Excuse me, please?

Caleb   Can't I say hello to your beloved?

Sol   Come out the way!

Davina   Stop it! You all right, Caleb?

Caleb   Yeah, I'm supercalifragilistic ex/piali—

Sol   MOVE!

Davina   Don't shout at your brother like that.

Agnes's Voice   What's going on in there?

Sol   Nothing, Mum!

Caleb   Sol's trying to bully me again!

Sol   You're such an idiot.

Davina   Sol?

Caleb   Don't worry, Davina, it's just sticks and stones. (*Tries to put his arm around* **Davina**.) So, to whom do I owe the pleasure of this visit?

Davina   I don't think so. Why are you wet?

Caleb   It's sweat, fresh sweat. You lot caught me in the middle of my training regime.

Sol (*laughs*)   Training regime?

Caleb   What? There's nothing wrong with keeping in shape. That's what real men do, Sol.

Sol   And what you trying to insinumate?

Caleb   The word's 'insinuate'.

Sol   Don't correct me.

Agnes's Voice   Solomon, I am making peanut soup, do you want some?

Caleb   No, he doesn't!

Sol *gives* **Caleb** *a look.* **Caleb** *smiles.*

Sol   Ermm (*To* **Davina**.) You hungry?

Davina   Sol, I didn't come here to eat peanut soup, we came here to . . . (*Sighs.*) Forget it . . .

Sol   Davina –

Davina   You're not taking this seriously!

Sol   I am . . .

Agnes's Voice   *Ah-ah*, whose voice is that?

Pause.

Sol   It's me, Mum. (*To* **Davina**.) Let me just check she's all right and then we'll talk to her.

Davina   I don't understand?

Sol   I just want to check she's in the right . . . mood.

Davina (*sighs*)   Where's your toilet?

Sol   Upstairs, first door on the right . . .

Caleb   I'll escort you if you want?

Sol *hits* **Caleb**.

Davina   Stop the violence!

Davina *goes upstairs.*

Caleb (*pokes **Sol***'s belly*)   That's the junk-food wobble right there.

Sol   Keep your hands to yourself.

Caleb   Does the truth hurt?

Sol   What truth? You're chatting foolishness!

Caleb   Am I?

Sol   Yes you are!

Agnes *comes into the room.*

Agnes   *Ah-ah*, don't start that nonsense in my house!

Sol   I was just about to come and see you in the kitchen.

Agnes   So you have come to fill your belly then go, is that it?

Sol   No, don't say that.

Agnes   Then why are you here?

Beat.

Sol   Have I got any letters?

Agnes   Check on the table.

Sol *begins to walk over the rug.*

Agnes   Shoes!

Sol   Yeah, sorry.

Sol *takes his shoes off and goes through the letters on the table.*

Agnes   Caleb, why are you wet?

Caleb   It's sweat.

Agnes   I hope you haven't been dripping on my beautiful, beautiful carpet?

Caleb   Don't worry, I haven't.

Sol   Yeah, Mum, erm . . . (*Beat.*) We need to talk . . .

Agnes   Ah, finally the day has come.

Sol   Eh?

Agnes   At last you've come to your senses and now want to talk business. Let me just get my glasses from upstairs and we can go through the paperwork for the house.

Caleb   Eh?

Sol   No, no, no, Mum, that's not why I came here.

Agnes   Solomon, I leave for Ghana in four weeks, I have no time for games!

Sol   Yeah, I know.

Agnes   So why are you here?

Sol   Erm . . . (*Sees one of his letters opened.*) Why is this open?

Caleb   Oh, if that's the one from your workplace, I opened it by mistake.

Sol   What?

Caleb   It was a mistake!

Sol   Mistake?! How can you open it by mistake?

Caleb   I was in a rush this morning. I'm a full-time working man.

Sol   Since when did the name Solomon look like Caleb?

Caleb   I'm a busy man! I got no time to be filtering through letters. Anyway it's about time you got them redirected to your new abode.

Agnes   Caleb, you shouldn't be opening your brother's letters.

Caleb   It was a mistake!

Agnes (*to* **Sol**)   So, is that all you are here for?

Beat. **Agnes** *kisses her teeth and goes towards the kitchen.*

Sol   Erm, well . . . (*Beat.*) Mum?

Agnes What?

Beat.

Sol I'll have some soup, if it's still all right?

Agnes (*kisses her teeth*) One minute.

She exits to the kitchen.

Caleb The cheek of the man.

Sol What?

Caleb Coming around here and eating my food, in my house! (*Attempts to kiss his teeth but fails.*)

Sol You didn't cook the food and this ain't your house!

Caleb Yet.

Sol You think she'll trust a kid like you, on your own, with the house?

Caleb I'm a professional man, working a professional job, earning a professional man's salary. Remind me what you do again?

Sol Don't question me.

Caleb Stacking shelves, ain't it? A good ol' shelf-stacker! How's the fruit section doing these days? Are the lemons still refusing to stay on the shelf?

Sol Whatever, man . . .

Caleb But then again, according to that letter, you're now suspended, aren't you? The suspended shelf-stacker from Sainsbury's. It's Sol, Sol sad.

Sol Don't try to make out like you're something cos you work in the city, Caleb. You're just a slave in a suit!

Caleb A slave in a suit?

Sol Yeah, that's right, a slave in a suit!

Caleb I'm shocked and appalled . . .

Sol   Why? Does the truth hurt?

Caleb   After all that our people have been through . . .

Sol (*laughs*)   What? This coming from the guy who said if he could have any actor in the world play his life story, he would choose Tom Hanks?

Caleb   He's an Oscar-winning superstar! I'm sorry if my preference isn't ghetto enough for you. Next time I'll just say Tupac, would that appease?

Sol   Tupac's dead, you fool!

Caleb   Well, that Biggie Smalls then.

Sol (*laughs*)   You are an idiot.

Caleb *throws his wet towel at* **Sol***.*

Sol   Why you trying it for you, *likkle eediat bwoy*! (*Kisses his teeth.*)

Caleb   'Likkle – eediat – bwoy', moi?

Sol *throws back the towel.*

Caleb   Aren't you worried that one day Davina will discover that you're not actually Jamaican?

Sol   Aren't you worried that one day your workplace will discover that you're not actually white?

Caleb (*sarcastically holds his chest*)   Ooooooooooo/ooooooooooo –

Sol (*mimics*)   'Ooooooooooo/ooooooooooo' –

Caleb   Ahhhhhhhh, your mum!

Sol   You got the same mum as me, you fool!

The two laugh. **Davina** *comes downstairs.*

Sol (*kisses his teeth*)   Eediat bwoy.

Davina (*to* **Sol**)   Oi!

Sol (*to* **Davina**)   What?

Davina   What did I say about talking to your brother like that?

Caleb   Yeah, listen to your woman!

Sol *goes to hit* **Caleb** *but misses.* **Davina** *holds him back.*

Davina   Stop it, Sol.

Sol   I'm just messing.

Davina   Look, can we just talk to your mum and get out of here, please?

Caleb (*jogging on the spot, to* **Sol**)   You want a piece of me?

Sol (*to* **Davina**)   You see that! He's always proaking me!

Caleb   Provoking!

Davina (*sighs*)   Is this what I'm gonna have to put up with in the future?

Sol   Don't worry, I'll send him to Ghana and let Mum take care of him.

Caleb   Maybe I'll send you to Ghana and I'll take care of Davina.

Davina *laughs. Enter* **Agnes**.

Sol   Yeah, whatever. Crazy kid.

Agnes   Solomon Joshua Kwabena Mensah! What is the meaning of this?

Sol   Meaning of what?

Agnes (*points to* **Davina**)   This!

Sol   Yeah, erm . . . We need to talk . . .

Agnes   Talk about what? I have nothing to say concerning her!

Sol   Well, I do.

Agnes   I said all I have to say about this one.

Sol   I know but –

Agnes   Are you hard of hearing?

Sol   No, Mum –

Agnes   Is she pregnant?

Davina   No!

Sol   Mum?

Davina   Agnes?

Agnes   Agnes?

Davina   Sorry, Mrs Mensah . . .

Agnes *kisses her teeth.*

Davina   Look, Sol and I have been discussing our future and –

Agnes   Solomon why did you bring this girl here again to my house?

Davina   Please, Mrs Mensah, I don't want to argue, we just wanted to talk –

Agnes   Can you remove yourself off my carpet!

Davina   Sorry. Mrs Mensah, there's only a month before you go and I'd . . . we would really appreciate it if there was any way we could reason or compromise. You don't have to like me but you can at least acknowledge that me and Sol are a couple.

Agnes   So now you come into my house and tell me what to do? Listen, er . . .

Sol   Davina.

Agnes   Davina. You are a reasonably beautiful girl. You still have time to find someone else and / maybe . . .

Davina   I don't want to find 'someone else'. I want to be with Sol!

Agnes   Just take your eyelids and your eye make-up and blink them at someone else.

Davina   But me and Sol / have . . .

Agnes   Solomon, do not allow this girl in my house while I am here, or while I am gone!

Davina   But –

Agnes   Out!

Davina   But –

Agnes   Now!

Davina   Please Mrs / Mensah –

Agnes   I said get off my carpet!

Davina   Sorry –

Agnes   Leave!

Davina   Please?

Agnes   Be gone from my house!

Davina   Sol?

Pause.

Sol   Look, Mum . . . (*Pause. To* **Davina***.*) You best wait in the car, yeah? I soon come.

Davina   I thought we were gonna do this together?

Sol   I'll handle this, okay?

Davina   But? (*Beat.*) I tried.

She walks out.

Sol   Mum, you had no right speaking to / her like . . .

Agnes   Now, Solomon, I'm giving you one more chance.

Sol   One more chance for what?

Agnes   You have no time to still be confused.

Sol   I never said I was confused about anything, Mum.

Agnes   I am in the last days before I retire. In four weeks I go to Ghana for good. But I am not leaving your junior brother in this house on his own . . .

Caleb   But / Mum . . .

Sol   Yes, and I agree . . .

Caleb   No, no, no – we've discussed this already – I am not sharing this house with him!

Agnes (*to* **Caleb**)   You have no say in the matter.

Caleb   But Mum . . .

Agnes   Solomon is your elder, full stop.

Caleb *sighs.*

Sol   But that's the thing, Mum, I got no problem moving back here and watching over Caleb, if that's what you want.

Caleb   I'm twenty-two, goddamit!

Agnes   *Uh-uh!* No blaspheming in my house!

Caleb   How's that blaspheming?!

Sol   But I can only move back in the house with Davina. She's my life now.

Agnes   You what?

Sol   So the two of us can watch over the place together.

Agnes   Us?

Sol   Yeah, me and Davina.

Agnes   You think I'd leave my beautiful, beautiful home of fifteen years to you and that . . . that . . . girl?

Caleb   *Innit,* you lost your marbles or something?

Sol   Shut up, *man!* This has got nothing to do with you!

Agnes   Don't tell him to shut up! He's involved too.

Caleb   Exactly!

Agnes (*to* **Caleb**)   Shut up! (*To* **Sol**.) Now listen, time is ticking fast. You can come home now and we can reconcile. I'll forgive all your waywardness and when I am gone you and your brother can enjoy this place. Or you can choose to go back to that . . . that . . . girl and don't bother coming back here again.

Sol (*sighs*)   Why won't you listen?

Agnes   I'm giving you one last chance to come home and leave that concubine-living behind!

Sol   Oh, here we go with the concubine-living . . .

Caleb (*smirks*)   Truth hurt?

Agnes   Keep quiet!

Sol   This is ridiculous!

Agnes   Make your decision!

Beat.

Sol   I don't know why you don't listen. I am twenty-six years old, this is the twenty-first century, I don't need your permission. I can live with whoever I want!

Agnes   But you're not bringing her into my house!

Sol   Well then, if that's the case, I don't want your house. Give it to Caleb, I don't care!

Caleb   Yessss!

Agnes   I brought you up better than this. I raised you with morals and values. How comes Caleb can keep in line but you had to go haywire?

Sol   Well, I'm sorry I ain't like Caleb!

He goes to exit.

Agnes   Do you really believe that girl can provide you er . . . stability, support, / loyalty –

Sol   Davina and me are gonna be together for ever whether you like it or not!

Agnes   Wake up, Solomon! This is the real world. I know those type of women, you can do so much better.

Sol   What do you mean those 'type' of women?

Agnes   You think she can look after you like I have? I've done this for twenty-plus years, on my own, Solomon, on my own!

Sol   I'm sorry, Mum. (*Beat.*) You take care, yeah?

He opens the door to leave.

Agnes   You don't need to do this. You know better, this is your home!

Beat.

What about the soup?

Sol *exits.* **Agnes** *sighs. Beat.* **Caleb** *goes to put his arm around* **Agnes**.

Caleb   Don't worry, Mum . . .

Agnes   Get your sweaty body away from me!

Caleb   I was just going to reassure you that in future you'll be much prouder of my choice in women, that's all.

Agnes   Caleb?

Caleb   Yes, Mother dear?

Agnes   Shut up!

Scene Two

Two weeks are left before **Agnes***'s departure.*

Night time. **Agnes***'s living room. All the house lights are off. A lamp post from outside lets in streaks of light across the rug and other parts of the room. A sound of the front door slamming hard against a wall is heard and we can just about see the two figures of* **Sol** *and* **Mehmet** *in the shadows, entering the room. A loud clang is heard of several metal objects falling on to the floor.*

Sol   What's wrong with you?

Mehmet   It ain't my fault!

Sol   I swear, if any of them are broken . . .

Mehmet   It will be your fault then, *innit*?!

Sol   How's it gonna be my fault?

Mehmet   Can't even pack properly . . .

Sol   That's got nothing to do with it. It's about you not looking where you're going!

Mehmet   How can I see where I'm going?!

More things begin to fall on the floor.

Ahh, *man*!

Sol   What's wrong with you?

Mehmet   It's your cheap box!

Sol   You're meant to hold it at the bottom where the / fold is . . .

Mehmet   I was holding it at the bottom, but the things still came through . . .

Sol   How can they go through your hands?

Mehmet   They didn't go through my hands, you fool, they went through the bottom of the box!

Sol   How can they go through the bottom of the box if your hands are there?

Mehmet   Because it's a cheap box!

Sol   You're going on like I bought the box from Oxfam or something.

Mehmet   You stole them from your workplace.

Sol   I didn't steal them, you idiot. It's my leaving present to myself.

Mehmet   From the bins?

Sol   Shut up, *man*.

The lights come on. We see **Caleb** *standing at the foot of the stairs at the light switch. He's wearing a Thundercats T-shirt and is in his boxers. He holds a baseball bat firmly in his hand.*

Caleb (*to* **Sol**)   What are you doing?

Mehmet   Sup, Caleb!

Sol   Go to bed!

Caleb   Really, what – are – you – doing? I thought someone was trying to break in!

Mehmet   So you thought you'd show them a bit of leg to scare them off, eh?

He laughs, but no one else joins in.

Caleb   What's going on?

Sol   Nothing – go to bed.

Caleb   Get off Mum's carpet!

Sol   What?

Caleb   Take your shoes off, you idiot!

Sol   Who you talking to? I'll knock you out, you know?!

Caleb   Just because you're my brother, don't think I would hesitate to call the police if you ever did!

Mehmet   Derr . . . How can you call the police if you're KO'ed on the floor? (*Laughs.*)

Caleb (*to* **Mehmet**)   And you, get out of my house!

Caleb *is ignored.* **Sol** *begins to unpack.* **Caleb** *snoops around* **Sol**'s *stuff.*

Caleb   If I'm not mistaken, it looks like you're trying to move back in. But I am mistaken, aren't I? You wouldn't be doing anything like that, would you? Of course not – you got your own place, haven't you? Haven't you?

No response.

Sol, please tell me you're not moving back in.

No response.

(*Sighs.*)   You can not be / serious –

Sol   If I wanna move back home, then I will.

Caleb   Oh, so this is your home now is it? (*Tuts.*) My, my, my . . . It took eleven months, but it finally happens. You couldn't even make it to the one-year mark. Mum was right.

Mehmet   All right, mate, leave it.

Caleb   I thought you knew what you were doing? It was only two weeks ago you were declaring how 'me and Davina are gonna be together for ever'! See, Mum was right.

Sol   If I was you, I'd stop talking . . .

Caleb   Why, does the truth hurt? What was it Mum called Davina again? Jezebel? Yeah, that was it – a jezebel! A right old jezzie!

Sol *goes for* **Caleb**.

Mehmet   All right, boys, chill. Caleb, why don't you help take some of your brother's stuff upstairs?

Caleb   Where?

Mehmet   To his room.

Caleb   He hasn't got a room any more. The only rooms upstairs are my room, Mum's room, the bathroom and my fitness room.

Mehmet   What?

Sol   He's packed out my room with his treadmill and his weights.

Caleb   But it's not your room, though. You relinquished the area when you left to shack up with that female.

Mehmet   But where you gonna put your stuff then?

Sol (*sighs*)   Just leave it here for now. I'll sort it out in the morning.

Mehmet   Where's your mum?

Sol (*to* **Caleb**)   She at work?

Caleb   Yeah.

Sol   Lend me a pillow then?

Caleb *lets out a loud, exaggerated sigh.*

Sol   I don't know why you're sighing.

Caleb   What's the magic word?

Sol   Now!

Caleb   Dear oh dear . . .

Sol   I'll just go upstairs and take all your pillows, if you're gonna be like that?!

Caleb   Oooo, look at you . . .

Sol   Don't test me, Caleb, I'm seriously not in the mood.

Caleb *goes upstairs.* **Sol** *walks* **Mehmet** *to the door.*

Mehmet   Again, sorry I couldn't take you in; I'm already walking a tightrope with my uncle.

Sol   It's cool, I don't want to get you in any problems.

Mehmet   If there was any other way . . .

Sol   It's all right bro, it's okay.

Mehmet   Can I trust you not to knock ten bells out of Caleb?

Sol   No promises, *blud*.

Beat.

Mehmet   Do you want me to speak to Davina for you? Try make her / see that –

Sol   Na, na, na – no need for that.

Mehmet   I've never seen Davina so angry. Come to think about it, I've never seen a woman so angry before.

Sol   That's females, *innit*. The same passion she had in throwing my things in the road will be the same energy she'll be using to make things up, trust me.

Mehmet   You sure?

Sol   Yes! Go home, get some sleep, *man*!

Mehmet   All right.

Sol   I'll catch you tomorrow.

Mehmet   All right, take it easy, yeah?!

Sol   Yeah, you too. And thanks for your help tonight, dropping me off home and that, appreciate it.

Mehmet   No worries, bro, later!

Sol   Later!

Mehmet *exits.* **Sol** *takes a moment to look around the living room. The realisation that he is back at his mother's house begins to set in. He slumps on to the sofa and takes a couple of deep breaths to control the growing feeling of frustration. A few tears begin to fall from his eyes.* **Caleb** *comes bouncing down the stairs with a couple of pillows under his arms.*

Caleb   Here you go. Have these two flat ones.

Caleb *throws the pillows at* **Sol***.* **Sol** *tries to clear his face.*

Caleb   What's the matter with you?

Sol   Hay fever. Thanks for the pillows, yeah?

Caleb   No problem.

He sits next to **Sol** *and stares at him.* **Sol** *turns his face.*

Sol   What you staring at?

Caleb   Just reading the signs.

Sol   What signs?

Caleb   The signs of heartache.

Sol (*sighs*)   You don't have to hang around, you know! You can go to bed.

Caleb   Maybe I want to spend some quality time with my big bro.

Sol   Quality time? (*Laughs.*)

Caleb   Yeah.

Sol   A few moments ago you were threatening to call police on me.

Caleb   Only cos you were threatening to smash my head in.

Sol   See how you always exaggerate!

Caleb   You were though!

Sol   Have I ever done it before?

Caleb   Can't remember.

Sol   So what makes you think I'm gonna do it now?

Caleb   I said I can't remember.

Sol   Course you would remember if I had smashed your head in before!

Caleb   Not necessarily, the blows might have caused memory loss.

Sol   Can you feel any dents on your head that might feel like it's ever been smashed in?

Beat.

Caleb   I might have had a good plastic surgeon.

Sol   Go to bed, *man.*

Pause. The silence is broken by **Caleb***'s laughter.*

Sol   What?

Caleb   Nothing . . . nothing . . .

Sol   What?

Caleb   No, I just remembered when your foot got stuck in the kitchen wall.

Sol   That kick was aimed for your head.

Caleb   You see, you are violent!

Sol   I never connected. (*Beat.*) You were always in need of discipline.

Caleb   You got more beats than me. Most times I just got my Mega Drive taken away. You used to get the Hoover pipe, the wooden spoon and the remote control thrown at your head – repeatedly.

Sol   That wasn't your Mega Drive, it was mine!

Caleb   I don't think you're remembering properly.

Sol   I think I am.

Caleb   Remember, Mum gave me your Mega Drive after she caught you sneaking out the house.

Beat. **Sol** *smiles to himself.*

Sol   Oh yeah.

Caleb   See.

Sol   Was still mine first.

Caleb   It doesn't matter how you begin but how you end.

Beat.

Sol   I guess that's what happens when you're the oldest. You get off so lightly, you know that?

Caleb   No, I don't.

Sol   Yes, you do, *man*.

Caleb   I never did anything major. I was a good boy.

Sol   A mummy's boy, you mean.

Caleb   No.

Sol *begins to take off his socks.*

Sol   I still got that scar on my toe, you know.

Caleb   Ah, the 'war wounds'. There's still the mark in the wall as well. It's probably a piece of your flesh. Poor wall.

Sol   Who cares about that stupid wall, I could have broken my foot!

Caleb   You shouldn't have been trying to kick me then.

Pause.

Caleb   You wanna see another 'war wound'?

He begins to lift his boxer shorts high above his thigh.

Sol   Close your legs, *man*, I don't want to see your *tingz*!

Caleb   No, you pervert, look!

Pointing to a dark line along the top of his thigh.

Caleb   The stripes of war. Remember this one?

Sol   No.

Caleb   Michael Jackson? The moonwalk?

Sol *shakes his head.*

Caleb   Table? Glass table?

Sol *shakes his head.*

Caleb   Birthday party?

Sol   Oh! (*Laughs.*) You talking about when it was my birthday party and you was acting the fool?

Caleb   You scarred me for life!

Sol   You scarred yourself for life.

Caleb   Who asked you to come on the table with me?

Sol   You were trying to copy my moves! I was the one who showed you that it was easier to do it on the table.

Caleb   Yeah, but I was the one who showed you how to do it properly.

Sol   That day went down as no contest.

Caleb   You couldn't take that I was getting all the attention on your birthday, so you tried to kill me!

Sol (*laughs*)   I told you to come off the table, but you didn't listen.

Caleb   I told you to wait your turn.

Sol   Why should I? I'm the oldest.

Caleb   A shame you're not the brightest. Any fool could see that table couldn't take two people – (*feels the scar*) and lo and behold –

Sol   Well, I got injured too.

Caleb   Sol, I think there's a difference between a cut toe and glass wedged in your thigh. I could have died!

Sol   You're going on like I intentantly set out to hurt you.

Caleb   Intentionally.

Sol   Shut up.

Caleb   Sol, I was seven years old!

Beat.

Sol   Well, I'm sorry, *innit*, if that's what you wanna hear – again.

Caleb   Don't worry, it's all part of the 'war wounds'.

Sol   War wounds?

Caleb   'War wounds' – a collection of scars and bruises from sibling rivalry.

Sol (*laughs*)   You're so weird.

Pause.

Caleb   But now I see you are wounded from wars on a different front.

Sol   What?

Caleb   Matters of the heart.

Sol   Yeah, well, one day you might know what it is to be with a real woman, and then you might actually know how it feels to be in love.

Caleb   Oh, I know all about women.

Sol   I'm sure you do, Caleb. But I'm talking about real women now, not the online type.

Caleb   If I was you, I'd listen. There's great wisdom carried in this twenty-two-year-old cranium.

Sol   Talk properly, *man*!

Beat.

Caleb   So why did she throw you out?

Sol   She didn't throw me out.

Caleb   So why did you leave?

Sol   It's none of your business.

Caleb   It is when you're seeking refuge in my house!

Sol   This ain't your house.

Caleb   Soon will be. (*Beat.*) I overheard your friend saying something about you stealing from Oxfam? I sincerely hope you haven't stooped that low . . .

Sol (*sighs*)   I'm not stealing from Oxfam . . . we were talking about boxes.

Caleb   Were you considering living in a cardboard box?

Sol   No, you idiot, I just got them from work to . . . (*Sighs.*)

Caleb   So you're here for good?

Sol   I'm / not . . .

Caleb   You better not be.

Sol   You really think I'd want to share a place with you? I'm only here temporary.

Caleb   Well, that's excellent news.

Beat.

Sol   Caleb, what is your problem?

Caleb   My problem, young Solomon, is that memories fade – (*points to his thigh*) but the scars still linger!

Sol   So you're still bitter over foolishness when we were kids?

Caleb   'War wounds'.

Sol   Whatever. That was all in the past. We're grown men now . . . Well, I'm a grown man, anyway.

Caleb   But hasn't the past taught you anything? Sol – we cannot abide together. We're like chalk and cheese, oil and water . . .

Sol   Black and white. (*Laughs.*)

Caleb   You're not funny, Sol. (*Gets up.*) You got two weeks!

Sol   I can stay here as long as I want . . .

Caleb   This ain't your house any more. You relinquished all rights of potential ownership in favour of your 'Caribbean queen'. Now I'm sorry that your gamble didn't pay off, but this is my house now, for my future and my family.

Sol   So what am I?

Beat.

Caleb   You got two weeks.

He exits upstairs. **Sol** *clears the sofa. He lies down and uses his jacket to cover what he can of his body.*

Scene Three

Next morning. Half of **Sol**'s *body is now hanging off the sofa.* **Agnes** *enters from outside and takes off her shoes. She sees that* **Sol**'s *stuff is everywhere and approaches him.*

Agnes   *Eh!*

Then she sees **Sol** *on the sofa.*

Agnes   SOLOMON?!

Sol *curls up and mumbles.*

Agnes   SOLOMON! WHAT IS THE MEANING OF ALL THIS?

Sol *groans as* **Agnes** *pulls his jacket off him.*

Agnes   I asked you a question.

Sol   Eh?

Agnes   I said, what is the meaning of all this?

Sol   Don't worry, I'll move it in a minute.

Agnes   You'll move it now! And who's been stepping on my carpet?

Sol   No one, Mum.

Agnes   I can see shoe prints all over.

Sol (*looks at the rug*)   Where?

Agnes   Did you bring that girl here? Where is she?

Sol   No, Mum, she ain't here.

Agnes   Then whose footprints are these?

Sol   It might be Mehmet's.

Agnes   Mehmet? What is he doing here?

Caleb *comes downstairs fully dressed ready for work, in a shirt and tie.*

Sol   He's not here now . . .

Agnes   I don't expect to come home from work to this nonsense!

Caleb   Oh dear, oh dear. I tried to wake him up earlier but he didn't want to know.

Sol   Why you lying for?

Agnes   So what is going on?

No response.

Well?

No response.

Solomon, I asked you a question!

Caleb   Davina kicked him out.

Sol   She didn't kick me out.

Caleb   What happen then?

Beat.

Sol   We're . . . on a break . . .

Caleb *laughs.*

Agnes   So you decide to go on a break in the middle of the night?

Sol   No . . . obviously we talked about it.

Caleb   Argued, more like.

Agnes   So she kicked you out?

Sol   No.

Agnes   What do you call it when you are forced to leave your home?

Caleb I'd call it an eviction. Did you know, Mum, Davina threw his stuff into the road?

Agnes *Eh?* She threw your stuff into the road?

Sol She was angry / and . . .

Agnes Angry? Angry about what? What did you do?

Sol Nothing.

Agnes So she threw your clothes out for no reason?

Sol No . . .

Agnes Well, what then?

Sol It doesn't matter.

Agnes It matters to me when you move back here without notice. See how you've destroyed my beautiful, beautiful carpet!

Sol I haven't destroyed it. I said I'll move all this in / a minute.

Agnes Caleb, start taking Sol's things into the spare room.

Caleb What spare room?

Agnes The room with all you weightlifting rubbish.

Caleb That's my fitness room! Na, sorry – he's gonna have to find somewhere else; all the spaces here are occupied.

Agnes It's rather there or I tell him to put it into your bedroom.

Caleb I can't believe this!

A car horn is heard. **Caleb** *heads for the exit.*

Agnes Caleb?

Caleb I'm going to work, Mum.

Agnes What time will you be home?

Caleb Dunno – but probably late. (*To* **Sol**.) And you, stay out my rooms!

He exits. Beat.

Agnes   Well, start taking your things upstairs.

Sol *begins to gather a few of his things.* **Agnes** *watches him. Beat.*

Agnes   At least I can now leave this country in peace. If you want I can make some soup later to celebrate.

Sol   Celebrate what?

Agnes   My prodigal son returning home. I hope you learnt your lesson and you listen to me from now on.

Sol   For the last time, we're on a break, / okay?

Agnes   The heartache will confuse your head for a few days, but you'll be back to normal soon.

Sol   I'm not confused. I'm telling you that we're on a break.

Agnes   Solomon, do not deceive yourself. Just be grateful that I have welcomed you back home.

Sol   Grateful?

Agnes   See, I know those types of girls. She'll be out there now looking for someone else to suck dry. I'm not judging her; I'm just speaking the truth.

Sol   For God's sake . . .

Agnes   *Ah-ah!* No blaspheming in my house! Just see yourself lucky that she got bored of you and moved on. If it was meant to be, then this would not have happen.

Sol   It was you, Mum! You messed up my relationship!

Agnes   What did I do?

Sol   How can you be so blind not to see what you were doing? How can you be so . . . so . . . (*Sighs.*)

He storms upstairs.

Agnes   Where are you going? Solomon? I asked you a question – where are you going?

There's a sound of a door slamming shut from upstairs.

Scene Four

Lunchtime. **Caleb** *and* **Michaela** *are in the park near their workplace.*

Caleb   So now my brother has moved back home, which has ruined my plans.

Michaela   What plans?

Caleb   For me to get the house.

Michaela   I'm sure they're not all ruined.

Caleb   It feels like it.

Michaela   How long is he staying for?

Caleb   He says he's just on a break, but I know she's kicked him out for good. I knew there was no way he could hold that relationship down without messing it up.

Michaela   Why do you say that?

Caleb   Because my brother ain't like me, we're totally different.

Michaela   I'd like to meet your brother.

Caleb   Why?

Michaela   To see if you guys look alike?

Caleb   We don't.

Michaela   Or if there are any other similarities?

Caleb   There isn't.

Michaela   Nah, you can't be that different?

Caleb   Trust me, we haven't got anything in common. For starters he takes more after my dad and I guess I take more after my mum.

Michaela   What do you mean?

Caleb   That child is reckless! He has no respect for my mum, or me. It's no surprise that his girlfriend kicked him out.

Michaela   You're just exaggerating now. He can't be that bad . . .

Caleb   How would you know? You don't know him.

Michaela   All right, all right. If you've got issues with your brother, don't take it out on me . . .

Caleb   I'm not . . .

Michaela   Just because you're more of a mummy's boy doesn't / mean that . . .

Caleb   No, I'm not . . .

Michaela   Yes, you are.

Caleb   No, I'm not.

Michaela   Don't worry, Caleb, I think it's sweet. It shows you care about your mother.

Caleb   Doesn't make me a 'mummy's boy' though.

Michaela *smiles. Beat.*

Michaela   Where is your dad anyway? . . . If you don't mind me asking?

Caleb   I dunno. Mum drove him out years ago.

Michaela   Do you miss him?

Caleb   You can't miss what you never knew.

Michaela   You sure?

Caleb   Yes. I mean – he left when I was, what? Three – four. So I can't remember much of him.

Michaela   That's sad.

Caleb   Yeah, well – such is life.

Beat.

Michaela   No stepfathers or anything?

Caleb   Erm . . . no!

Michaela   What about that other man you were talking about earlier, your uncle?

Caleb   What, Uncle Godfrey?

Michaela   Yeah.

Caleb   He ain't my uncle. Just my mum's friend from church.

Michaela   So it's been just you, your mum and your brother?

Caleb   Me, my mum and Sol.

Beat.

Michaela   I could never imagine not having my dad. Gosh, I don't know what I'd do without him. That's why I didn't move too far from home, just in case I might need him for anything. I can call him up and be like, 'Dad there's a spider in my bathroom,' and I know he'll be around straight away.

Caleb   Daddy's girl, eh?

Michaela   Yep!

Caleb   Got him wrapped around your finger?

Michaela   Yep!

Caleb   Even at the grand old age of thirty?

Michaela *hits* **Caleb**.

Caleb (*laughs*)   Sorry – twenty-nine.

Michaela   Rudeness. And by the way, my daddy's very protective of me, so you better be careful, mate!

Caleb   Don't worry – if I ever see a skinhead, middle-aged man running towards me, I'll know what to do.

Michaela   He hasn't got a skinhead.

Caleb   Well, any middle-aged Caucasian male then.

The two laugh. Beat.

Michaela   I think it's really sad.

Caleb   What's sad?

Michaela   About your dad.

Caleb (*laughs*)   Honestly, I'm all right – I've still managed to grow up to be a man, haven't I? I've graduated from uni, I've got a job in a good company and soon I'll have my own house. All this without having him around. Not bad, eh?

Michaela   But you could have brothers and sisters out there, walk past them and never know who they were.

Caleb   Hmm . . . I have actually thought of that before. To think I could be eyeing up a woman across the road who potentially could be my half-sister. (*Shudders.*) It's a good thing I only like white women. Safety.

The two laugh.

Michaela   But don't you want someone more like your mummy, since you claim you're more like her?

Caleb   Urgh! I love my mum, but I don't wanna marry someone like her, that ain't right.

Michaela   So who would be the ideal person that you would wanna marry?

Caleb   Like you don't already know.

Michaela   Remind me . . .

Caleb *kisses* **Michaela**.

Caleb   Mmm . . . Scarlett Johansson.

Michaela *hits* **Caleb** *and he laughs.*

Michaela   You're so cruel, you know that? I don't know why I bother with you sometimes . . .

Caleb (*begins to sing*)   'Cos you lurve me, you really lurve me . . . '

Michaela   Go away, you don't treat me right.

Caleb   Yes I do.

He tries to kiss her but she shields her face.

You know I do . . .

Michaela   Stop it – people are looking.

Caleb   I don't care. I want the whole world to know about how much I love you.

Michaela   Except your mum?

Caleb   Hmm?

Michaela   When are you gonna tell your mum about us?

Caleb   Hmm?

Pushes **Caleb** *off.*

Michaela   When are you going to tell your mum about us?

Caleb   You know it's difficult at the moment. Plus her going away has made things especially tricky.

Michaela   Exactly, she won't be here for ever.

Caleb   I know, I know. But don't worry – it will be soon, I promise.

Michaela   You've been saying that for the last seven months.

Caleb   And I will.

He tries to kiss **Michaela** *but she turns away.*

Michaela   I don't understand why you don't tell her. You make me feel like I'm your dirty little secret.

Caleb   You're not, hun . . .

Michaela   Then tell her! Let's you and me go tell her together, tonight.

Caleb   We can't do that.

Michaela   Why not, Caleb?

Caleb   We can't, not tonight.

Michaela   This is getting beyond a joke now. I thought you were serious about me?

Caleb   I am.

Michaela   Are you ashamed of me?

Caleb   Course not. Why would you say that?

Michaela   Cos everything is so covert with you. Even a simple thing like picking you up in the morning, you won't even let me come to your doorstep!

Caleb   But there's no point . . . cos I'm coming out anyway.

Michaela   And you want me to move in with you? You make me laugh.

Caleb   I do. It's just . . . you just need to be patient, that's all. I want everything to be perfect when I do it. It has to be the right time.

Michaela   But I thought you said she was leaving in a couple of weeks? Time's running out.

Caleb   I promise you'll get to meet her before she goes, don't worry.

Michaela *sighs.*

Michaela   I guess we may as well go back to work then.

Caleb   Michaela, don't be like that.

Michaela   You know, Caleb, I don't care about whether or not you want me to move in with you, but I'm not prepared to be messed around.

Caleb   I'm not . . .

Michaela   I've even offered you the chance to meet my family, but I guess you're too scared . . .

Caleb   No, I am not scared. It just needs to be the right time, that's all.

Michaela   Well my patience is running out (*checks watch*) and I gotta get back to my desk.

Caleb   Michaela?

Scene Five

Early afternoon. **Mehmet**'s *uncle's chip shop.* **Mehmet** *is working behind the till and* **Sol** *is on the other side, watching him.*

Sol   That looks really good. (*Beat.*) Nothing like the smell of fish and chips. (*Beat.*) Even them savaloys, look good and I don't even eat pork. All red and juicy . . . (*Beat.*) You guys use Maris Piper potatoes, *innit*? I heard they make the best chips. (*Looks up to the menu on the wall.*) You do chicken as well? Quarter, half . . . whole? You can get a whole chicken and chips? That's a feast, *boi*. (*Beat.*) Steak and kidney pie, chicken and mushroom pie, beef and / onion –

Mehmet   Sol?

Sol   Yeah?

Mehmet   You gonna stand there and read about food all day?

Sol   Na . . . just interested.

Mehmet *serves some chips and gives them to* **Sol**.

Mehmet   Here ya, on the house.

Sol   Ah, *bless, bless, bless, bless, bless, bless, bless.*

He takes the food and begins to eat four chips at a time.

Mehmet   Slow down, bro, you'll get indigestion.

Sol   Haven't eaten all day.

Mehmet   You could have fooled me.

Sol   I couldn't stay in that house with that woman.

Mehmet   What woman?

Sol   My mum.

Mehmet (*shakes his head*)   It's only natural though, *innit*. She wants to check her son is okay.

Sol   Na, she just wants to check it's over between me and Davina. I'm not gonna give her that satisfaction, though.

Mehmet   You can't hang around the chip shop all day.

Sol   Yeah, I know.

Beat.

Mehmet   How's the job hunting going?

Sol   Hmm . . .

Mehmet   What's 'hmm'?

Sol   'Hmm' means 'hmm', *innit*!

Mehmet   No luck then? Or you haven't been looking?

Sol   Course I been looking. I know someone that works in a warehouse, said he'd get back to me later.

Mehmet   Is that it?

Sol   No.

Mehmet   Well, what else then?

Sol   What is this?

Mehmet   What? I'm just asking.

Sol   It's like you're 'terrogating me.

Mehmet   I'm not interrogating you. I'm just asking.

Sol   Yeah, well, I don't need the questioning right now.

Mehmet   If I can't check up on you, who can?

Sol   You're not my mum, or my woman.

Mehmet   Fine, whatever – have it your way.

Beat.

Sol   For your information, I got many things in the pipeline. Just need some time to get things established, gather some money together.

Mehmet   Ain't that whole point of getting a job?

Sol   What?

Mehmet   You get a job to get money.

Sol   Yeah, I know, but there's no point me just getting any old job. I may as well get started with what I've always wanted to do.

Mehmet   Yeah, but how you gonna do that with no money?

Sol   Yeah, that's why I need to get things rolling.

Mehmet   Yeah, but how you going to get things rolling if you don't have the money?

Sol   Yeah but . . . (*Beat.*) You make things so difficult.

Mehmet   I'm not making anything difficult – you're not making sense. You can't start anything without some money behind you.

Sol   I know that.

Mehmet   So where you gonna get money from in the mean time?

Sol   I dunno. I can get a bank loan or something . . . or a credit card.

Mehmet   With no job?

Sol   I've seen them adverts on TV saying I can consolomate all my debts.

Mehmet   Consolidate?

Sol   Don't correct me.

Mehmet   But that's for home-owners, something you ain't!

Sol   Yeah, I know.

Mehmet   Your little brother will be, though, *innit*?

Sol   Will be what?

Mehmet   A home-owner.

Sol   Don't remind me.

Mehmet   Maybe you can get him to cut you a deal.

Sol   I'd rather live on the streets than negotiate with that boy.

Mehmet (*laughs*)   How comes?

Sol   He's too devious. He'll be throwing in all sorts of terms and conditions.

Mehmet   But it's your brother, though, surely he'll allow you to stay at the house to give you time to get yourself sorted?

Sol   No, no, no – don't trust him, never have, never will.

Mehmet   But he's your brother, though . . .

Sol   No, I don't negotiate with terrorists!

Mehmet   Terrorist?

Sol   Since he was young he's always had a vendetta against me. He has always been Mum's little informer as well, always running to her and telling tales.

Beat.

Mehmet   But your mum will always be your mum. Surely she can help you out . . .

Sol   I don't want her help. If she can't accept Davina, then I don't want to know.

Mehmet   But in couple of weeks your mum's gone, where you gonna go then?

Sol   Things are only temporary. (*Holds out his mobile phone.*) Davina will call and everything will go back to normal.

Beat.

Mehmet   She ain't called then?

Sol   Not yet.

Mehmet   Have you called her?

Sol   *Bare* times, and she ain't picking up.

Mehmet   You tried calling her on private number?

Sol   Mehmet, I've tried everything. I've been around there *nuff* times and she ain't answering the door either.

Mehmet   I don't understand. You guys seem to be going really well, like. I mean, I know it can't be easy now that you ain't working . . .

Sol   It's more than me not having a job, Mehmet. I've got a mother who feels no way in telling my girlfriend how much she hates her. How long would you stay around if that always happened to you?

Mehmet   But you're a big man now and Davina's a big woman, it should be plain sailing for you two . . .

Sol   Big people still have problems, you know?! Age don't mean nothing, *man*. And the one problem in my relationship right now is my mum.

Mehmet   Well . . . just ride it out till she goes then.

Sol   If it was that easy do you think I'd even bother making effort? Davina was asking about how things are gonna be in future. Like at Christmas, what's it gonna be like then? If we got married – how's the wedding going to work? If we had kids, is my mum even gonna acknowledge them?

Mehmet   But all them things, yeah, you don't know how it will all play out till it happens.

Sol   But how my mum's carrying on now tells me that things in the future will be the same, if not worse. Mehmet, you don't understand, my mum's crazy!

Mehmet   Don't say that, *man*, you're just upset, that's all . . .

Sol   Nah, nah, nah – don't get it twisted, I love my mum yeah – but she crazy.

Mehmet   Don't worry about it for now, bro, you gotta do things little by little. But first thing first, you gotta focus on getting your woman before someone swipes her from under your nose.

Sol   Like who?

Mehmet   Don't look at me. You know I prefer light-skin girls anyway.

Sol   You need to grow out of that narrow-mindedness, *man*. There's a whole lot of women you're missing out on.

Mehmet   You just focus on your business, yeah, and I'll focus on mine.

Beat.

Sol   I'm sure she'll call any minute now, anyway, I can sense it. It's only a matter of time. I ain't worried, I ain't worried at all. Do I look worried to you?

Looks to **Mehmet** *for a response.*

Sol   You're meant to say 'no'.

Mehmet   Sorry, bro. No, you don't look worried.

Sol   I don't know why I bother with you sometimes.

Mehmet   Cos right now, I'm all you got!

Beat. **Sol** *looks at his mobile phone and sighs.*

Sol   I'll give her one more week.

Scene Six

One week left before **Agnes** *leaves.*

Early evening. **Caleb** *and* **Michaela** *are walking in* **Caleb**'s *local park.*

Caleb   How long you think it will be before Stuart gives me a promotion?

Michaela   I'm sure if you keep showing potential, it will be only a matter of time.

Caleb   Keeping his cup full of coffee, you mean?

Michaela   That too. But you got to start from somewhere.

Caleb   Yeah, but I didn't spend fifteen grand on a degree to photocopy all my life!

Michaela   Just be patient, things don't happen overnight. You got to remember, positions only come available when people leave.

Caleb   Well, Stuart should create a new position for me then. Make me assistant managing director or something. Suggest that to him at the next monthly meeting.

Michaela (*sarcastic*)   Yeah, I will.

Beat.

Caleb   How many people did you say done my role before I came?

Michaela   There were eight in the year before you.

Caleb   Eight?

Michaela   But most of them were temps.

Caleb   I was about to say. Sounded like some bad judgement in recruiting by the HR Department.

Michaela   What you trying to say, Caleb?

Caleb   Nothing.

Michaela   I've been in HR for two years and I think I've done a good job.

Caleb   So do I. I mean, after all, you employed me.

Michaela   Yes, I did, but that was only because you met the criteria, no other reason.

Caleb   And what was 'the criteria'?

Michaela   Erm . . . you were young, vibrant –

Caleb   Charismatic.

Michaela   – had good interpersonal skills –

Caleb   Charming.

Michaela   – showed an aptitude to learn things quickly –

Caleb   Intelligent.

Michaela   – unique individual . . .

Caleb   And black.

Michaela (*laughs*)   What's that got to do with anything?

Caleb   Every workplace has an ethnic quota to fill. It's the law, *innit?*

Michaela   Erm . . . It's complicated, but you were different. You were employed under my own personal criteria.

Caleb *laughs.*

Caleb   So you had this all planned out, didn't you?

Michaela (*laughs*)   No.

Caleb   You were using the interviewing process to speed date!

Michaela (*laughs*)   No!

Caleb   I knew you were eyeing me up in that interview. You couldn't care less about qualifications. I could have left school at aged twelve and you would have still employed me.

Michaela   But if you did, how would you have been able to build up that sexy vocab that seduces me every day?

Caleb   My vocabulary is built on years of non-stop television viewing, constant broadsheet reading and frequent thesaurus usage. So school had nothing to do with it.

Michaela   But it's not just what you say, it's the sound of your voice.

Caleb   What about it?

Michaela   It soothes me.

Caleb   … Okay.

Michaela   Don't get all funny on me.

Caleb   I'm not . . . I'm just thinking about what you said.

Michaela   I wish I didn't tell you now.

Caleb   How comes?

Michaela   Cos your head is beginning to block out the sun!

Caleb (*laughs*)   No, it's not.

Michaela   Big head!

Caleb   Don't you start with all that.

Michaela   What?

Caleb   My mum likes to remind me how much of a struggle it was to bring me into the world because of my, my – head.

Michaela (*looking at* **Caleb***'s head*)   Yeah . . . I really feel for her.

Caleb   Stop it.

Michaela *laughs. Beat.*

Michaela   I think me and your mum will get on really well.

Caleb   You do?

Michaela   Yeah, I mean going from what you've said about her, we sound similar.

Caleb   You are?

Michaela   Yeah. She sounds like a strong, assertive woman who cares about her children. I think we'll get along just fine.

Caleb   Yeah . . . I guess so.

Michaela   And that's why I need to meet her before she goes. It's only respectful and if I was her I would definitely want to know. Plus, I want to make sure that I get off on the right foot with her. I don't want her thinking I'm corrupting her sweet little boy.

Caleb   Yeah . . .

Beat.

Michaela   Are you all right?

Caleb   Yeah, yeah . . . just thinking. Seven months . . .

Michaela   I know. It feels like I've known you for ages.

Caleb   Yeah . . .

Michaela   We're gonna have so much fun in the future. Sometimes I daydream and get carried away, imagining what it's going to be like for us.

Caleb   You sound like a schoolgirl.

Michaela   So what?! Not all of us have had dozens of partners in life, you know?! I've never been with someone who cares about me as much as you say you do. And that means a lot to me. So I think I'm entitled to daydream as much as I want, don't you think?

Caleb   Yeah, sure . . . go for it.

Michaela   I dream about romantic holidays, the wedding day, kids . . .

Caleb   Wedding? Kids?

Michaela   Not now, silly – you need to get promotion or something first, like you said. But I can see them now – our little brown babies running around.

Caleb   Brown babies?

Michaela   Yeah. They'll have my beauty and probably your cheekiness.

She laughs, **Caleb** *watches her.*

Michaela   All right, I'll stop . . . for now. What places are around here to get something to eat?

Caleb   Why?

Michaela   I'm hungry, silly.

Caleb   There's a Chinese over there.

Michaela   Urgh . . . Don't eat Chinese, don't trust their food.

Caleb *looks at* **Michaela**.

Michaela   What? I had food poisoning a few years back after eating their food.

Caleb   What about Indian?

Michaela   Nah, don't eat their food either. I can't stand all that spicy stuff, it makes me feel sick. Haven't you got a chippie anywhere around here?

Caleb   The only one I know of is round the corner from mine.

Michaela   Let's go then.

Caleb   It's too hot for chips . . .

Michaela   I don't care, I'm hungry.

Caleb   Hmm . . .

Michaela   What?

Caleb   Just trying to think if there is another one nearby.

Michaela   What's wrong with your one?

Caleb   Not sure if it's open yet.

Michaela   It's five o clock!

Caleb   Yeah, I know . . .

Michaela   Stop being silly then, and come on.

Michaela *heads off in the direction of the chip shop and* **Caleb**
follows.

Scene Seven

Sol *enters the living room from outside. He realises he is stepping on the
rug and begins to remove his shoes. He loosens his shirt and tie and places
his CDs on the sofa. He brings out his mobile phone and begins to dial,
but a ring at the doorbell stops him. He walks to the door and opens it.*

Sol (*laughs*)   I was just about to call you . . .

Davina   One – do you think I enjoy my phone being plagued
by voice messages, text messages and missed calls? Two –
(*throws a plastic bag of underwear inside*) do you think that I want
your dirty socks lingering around my flat as a constant reminder
of you and your smelly feet? Three – do you think I appreciate
your greasy friends coming up to me, asking about our
business?

Sol   I didn't tell anyone to / talk to you . . .

Davina   Four – it's the end of the month and I still haven't
received your rent contribution / for the last three months!

Sol   Can you keep it down, my mum / is sleeping!

Davina   Five – (*pushes* **Sol**) who do you think you was
barging when you left?

Sol   I didn't barge you / when . . .

Davina   You pushed me!

Sol   I was walking and you were in the / way!

Davina   Six – what did you do with the Sky remote?

Sol *laughs.*

Davina   Don't laugh!

Sol   Oh yeah, I kinda took that with me by mistake.

Davina   I don't think it's funny. It's bad enough that you've been watching TV for free all these months, but when you leave, you ruin it for the rest!

Sol   I didn't mean to take it. It was a mistake, you / were rushing me . . .

Davina   What do you mean, a mistake? I threw your things outside. That was the only stuff you needed to concern yourself with. About your stealing the remote control – (*Kisses her teeth.*)

Sol   All right, all right, well, maybe I should go back over there and claim back my fridge?

Davina   I don't see how you can.

Sol   You don't think I will?

Davina   But I've changed locks so you can't get back in.

Sol *grabs* **Davina***'s keys from her hand.*

Sol   Not a problem.

Davina   I mean they're being changed as we speak.

Sol   You were always a bad liar.

Davina   How am I lying?

Sol   Cos you start blinking at a rapid pace.

Davina   No, I don't.

Sol   See, you're doing it now!

Davina   You must think I've come here for conversation.

Sol   Then leave, *innit.*

Davina   Not until you give me my money, Sol!

Sol   I've told you the situation, babes.

Davina   Don't 'babes' me – there ain't no 'babes' between us any more.

Sol   Look, I'll try my best to get something to you by the end of next week / and I'll –

Davina   Next week? You really must think I got 'stupid' written on my forehead?

Sol   You're not being fair now. / I've – (*Sighs.*)

Davina   I'm not being fair? Who's the one that's claimed they been suspended from their job to cover up the fact that they been sacked?!

Sol   I've been calling you every day but get no answer! Every time I try to get into the house, the door is bolted shut . . . I was suspended!

Davina   But at first you said to me you was on holiday –

Sol   I was on holiday. That's when I found out that I'd been suspended.

Davina   – and then you said you were suspended, and now you've lost your job. It's just one lie after another with you!

Sol   I'm not lying now, it's the truth!

Davina   Well, that's not gonna help me pay the rent this month, is it?

Sol   Look, Davina . . .

Davina   Ah, I don't wanna hear it, Sol, not any more.

Sol   So it's just about the money for you, is it? Because of money you're just gonna throw eleven months of relationship out the window?

Davina   And the lies, Sol. Don't forget about the lies, cos that's all you were doing. You just had to lie –

Sol   Oh, come on, Davina, like you haven't lied to me in the last year!

Davina   – and lie and lie and lie and lie some more.

Davina   I'm going . . .

Sol *grabs* **Davina***'s arm.*

Sol Are you really just gonna throw everything away because of money?

Davina Sol, let go of me . . .

Sol I'm sorry I didn't tell you the truth about my job, okay? And I'm sorry I ain't earning seventeen grand a year like you, but I am trying . . .

Davina Just leave me alone, Sol . . .

Sol I refuse to believe that it's because of money that you don't wanna be with me any more . . .

Davina Sol . . .

Sol Davina?

Davina What?

Sol I know you . . .

Davina No, you don't . . .

Sol Yes, I do. Look at me. (*Beat.*) Look at me.

Davina *looks at* **Sol**.

Sol Tell me what the problem is?

Davina Nothing.

Sol Do you still love me?

Davina What's that got to do with anything?

Sol Cos if you still love me, tell me the truth.

Davina A minute ago you were calling me a liar!

Sol No, look . . . please, Davina. If this is gonna be the end, at least tell me the real reason why you don't wanna be with me. (*Beat.*) Please.

Pause.

Davina Sol . . . Sol . . . (*Beat.*) Don't worry about it . . .

Sol *sighs. Beat.*

Davina   What's with the shirt and tie?

Sol   Job interview.

Davina   Oh . . . How'd it go?

Sol   All right, I guess.

Davina   When do you find out if you got it?

Sol   Dunno.

Davina   Where's it for?

Sol   Tesco's.

Davina   Oh . . . from Sainsbury's to Tesco's. (*Beat.*) Well . . . good luck . . .

Sol   Good luck?

Davina   Yeah.

Sol   Good luck? Is that the best you can do?

Davina   Well, what do you want me to say?

Sol   Davina . . . Davina, I'm trying my best to fix up. Do you think I liked you paying for everything? (*Sighs.*) Sorry . . . Look . . . you're the best thing to ever happen to me. I've never met anyone / like you –

Davina   Ah . . . Don't tell me that. Tell your mum!

Sol   My mum?

Davina   I can't do it any more, Sol, I can't do it. I can't take her any more! I know it's your mum and everything, but I can't . . . I can't . . .

Sol   I know it's hard for you . . .

Davina   How do you know? My mum has never called you a witch!

Sol   She was just joking when / she said –

Davina   And to top it off you never, ever support me when she attacks!

Sol   Now hold on, yes, I do . . .

Davina   When? Every time it happens you just stand there like a little boy.

Sol   You don't know what I've been through in this house defending you . . .

Davina   Well, it can't be that bad, since it's the first place you ran to when I kicked you out!

Pause.

Sol   Look . . . what does it matter now, anyway? She's gone next week / and we –

Davina   She might be going but she'll never be gone. Her words – (*points to her head*) will still be in here. And you want me to move in with you, into this place? Where her mark is everywhere . . . her smell . . . her aurora, even that stupid rug.

Sol   Well, I don't know what to do then, Davina. I don't.

Beat.

Davina   Sol . . . look . . . I accept that she will always be your mum. There's nothing I can do about that. And I'm not trying to make you choose between us . . .

Sol   Are you sure?

Davina   Yes . . . (*Beat.*) I don't know. (*Beat.*) All I know is that our relationship didn't . . . doesn't . . . have room for a third person.

Beat.

Sol   I know. (*Beat.*) And I'm sorry.

Pause.

Davina   How is your mum, anyway?

Sol   She's . . .

Agnes   I'm fine, thank you.

Agnes *comes into the living room wearing a nightgown and a headscarf.*

Agnes (*to* **Sol**)   What is she doing in my house?

Sol   Davina was just returning / my –

Agnes   I don't want her in my house!

Sol   She's not doing / anything wrong –

Agnes   How many times have I warned you Solomon, eh? / How many times –

Sol   Why don't you / ever listen –

Agnes   I've warned you a thousand times about bring this Jezebel into my house!

Davina (*looks at her watch sarcastically*)   Ahh, that train's never late . . .

Sol (*to* **Agnes**)   Why do you have to talk to her like that?

Davina   I'm gonna go, Sol.

Sol   Don't go, not yet.

Davina   Just . . . just think about what I said, okay?

Sol   You don't have to go.

Agnes   Yes, she does, she's unwelcome here.

Sol   Davina, wait!

Davina *exits.* **Sol** *storms past his mother and exits.*

Agnes   Eh! Who are you pushing? (*Beat.*) Solomon? SOLOMON?

Scene Eight

Evening. The chip shop. **Mehmet** *is currently working hard behind the till.* **Michaela** *enters first, followed by* **Caleb**.

Michaela (*looking up at the menu*)   Mmm . . . I don't know what I want now.

Caleb   I think I'm just gonna get some chips.

Michaela   You so boring!

Caleb   Nope, just sensible.

Beat.

Michaela   I dunno what I want now . . .

Caleb   Just get some chips!

Michaela   I don't want just chips!

Mehmet   Hi, can I help you? (*Sees* **Caleb**.) Caleb? You all right, mate?

Caleb   Yeah, I'm okay, thanks.

Mehmet   I heard you managed to keep your fitness room.

Caleb   Yeah . . .

Mehmet   Unlucky for Sol, eh?

Caleb   Yeah . . . yeah.

Beat.

Michaela (*to* **Caleb**)   Aren't you going to introduce me to your friend?

Caleb   Yeah . . . yeah.

Slight beat.

Michaela   Well?

Caleb   Erm . . . (*He takes his mobile phone from pocket.*) Oh, my phone.

Michaela   I didn't hear anything.

Caleb   I felt it vibrate – one sec . . .

He walks aside and 'checks' his mobile phone.

Michaela (*to* **Mehmet**)   Hi, I'm Michaela.

Mehmet   That's a pretty name for a pretty lady.

Michaela   Ah, I bet you say that to all your customers.

Mehmet   Only to the pretty ones.

Michaela (*laughs*)   You better stop that before you get my boyfriend jealous.

Mehmet   Boyfriend?

Michaela *looks at* **Caleb**, **Caleb** *looks at* **Michaela**, **Mehmet** *looks at* **Caleb**, **Caleb** *looks back at* **Mehmet** *and smiles.*

Mehmet   And a lucky man he is.

Caleb (*to* **Michaela**)   So what do you want?

Michaela   That was a quick call.

Caleb   It was a text, 'dear'.

Mehmet   So how long have you two been going out?

Caleb   Er . . . not that / long . . .

Michaela   Seven months, two weeks next Thursday.

Mehmet   Wow, ain't that nice?

Michaela   Yeah.

Mehmet   Your mum must be proud, eh, Caleb?

Caleb   Yep. (*To* **Michaela**.) I'm just gonna have chips, what do / you want –

Mehmet   I mean, to have such a beautiful woman on your arm. You'd want to tell the world about her.

Caleb   Not really. Some things I like to keep to myself, before it gets spoilt by others.

Michaela (*to* **Mehmet**)   Ignore him, he's just very possessive and wants me all to himself, don't you, hun?

Caleb   Yep. Can I have a small portion of chips please? (*To* **Michaela**.) What you having?

Michaela   Large cod and chips, please?

Caleb   Are you sure?

Michaela   Yes!

Mehmet   That will be around three minutes – is that okay?

Michaela   Yeah, that's fine.

Caleb *sighs.*

Michaela (*to* **Caleb**)   What?

Mehmet   So tell me how you found this goddess?

Caleb   Haven't you got a fish to fry?

Mehmet   All in good time, my friend, all in good time.

He puts a piece of cod in the fryer and goes to the back.

Michaela   What's the matter?

Caleb   Nothing?

Michaela *sees* **Caleb** *is still playing with his mobile phone.*

Michaela (*grabs the phone*)   Gimme this . . .

Caleb   What you doing?

Michaela (*checking the phone*)   What you doing?

Caleb   Don't be checking through my phone.

Michaela   There's obviously something important in here, more important than me . . .

Caleb (*grabs back the phone*)   Stop it!

Michaela   I was only playing.

Caleb   You have no right to check through my phone.

Michaela   You got something to hide?

Caleb   I've got nothing to hide. But you have no right to look through my phone!

Michaela   I have no right?

Caleb   No, you don't!

Mehmet *returns.*

Mehmet   So, Michaela? Caleb? How did you two meet?

Pause.

Don't all rush to answer now.

Michaela (*to* **Caleb**)   Why don't you tell the story, 'dear'.

Beat.

Caleb   Just . . . through . . . life, *innit.*

Mehmet   What?

Caleb   Through life . . . You meet people.

Mehmet   Ahh . . . you're not willing to reveal the details then?

Michaela   Nah, he wouldn't do that, he's too embarrassed. (*To* **Caleb**.) Aren't you, 'dear'?

Caleb   Embarrassed of what, Michaela?

Michaela   Embarrassed of me! Embarrassed of us!

Caleb   No . . .

Michaela   What is it then, regrets?

Caleb   It ain't regrets either . . .

Michaela   Well, what then? Why you look so pissed off?

Caleb   I'm just thinking, all right . . .

Michaela   Thinking about what, Caleb?

Caleb   Don't worry.

Michaela   No, I will worry, Caleb, cos you're getting on my nerves.

Caleb   Well, that makes two of us then!

Michaela   Ahh . . . the truth finally comes out. What else you been thinking, Caleb?

Caleb   Honestly?

Michaela   Yeah, honestly . . .

Caleb   I'm thinking how the hell did I end up in this!

Michaela   In what?

Caleb   In this! With you!

Michaela   I don't understand . . .

Caleb   Oh, come on, Michaela, this ain't serious!

Michaela   I am!

Caleb   This could never work on a long-term basis. This is foolish! The whole thing – it's foolish!

Michaela   I thought you were serious about everything . . .

Caleb   I was . . . up to a point. I just wanted to have fun. But you turned this all serious. Talking about meeting my mum, weddings, babies . . .

Mehmet   Babies?

Michaela   But why didn't you just say something when I was talking / that you –

Caleb   How was I suppose to say it? Whatever way I would have said it, you'd still react the same.

Michaela   So you decided to just play along with things, watching me get carried away like a fool . . .

Caleb   No! You don't understand, it wasn't like that at all. It was just that . . . that . . . that . . . that . . .

Michaela   You don't stutter, Caleb, be a man and say what you have to say!

Caleb   What I was going to say was . . . that . . . I've never known any woman on earth . . . so into me . . . to love me as much . . . as you do.

Michaela   That's meant to make me feel better, is it?

Caleb   But that's the thing. Because I knew this, and because you've been so nice to me, I couldn't / let –

Michaela (*sighs*)   Well, Michaela, what did you expect from a twenty-one-year-old?!

Caleb   I'm twenty-two!

Michaela   But you're obviously still acting like a child!

Caleb (*sighs*)   Just forget it, Michaela, it's over! I've got nothing more I want to say to you.

Michaela   Caleb?

Caleb *heads towards the exit.*

Caleb   It's over! Just leave me alone!

Michaela   Go on then, run off to your mummy! It must be bedtime soon!

Caleb   Sticks and stones, Michaela, sticks and stones!

Michaela   Aww . . . Is that what they taught you in nursery? Aww, bless.

Caleb   Well, if I'm some nursery kid, you must be really desperate, you bloody paedophile!

He leaves the chip shop. Pause.

Mehmet   Salt and vinegar?

Scene Nine

Evening. **Sol** *is pacing up and down the living room, holding his mobile phone.* **Agnes** *comes down the stairs, dressed immaculately in traditional robe.*

Agnes   So, what do you think?

No response.

Solomon?

No response.

SOLOMON?

Sol *stops and looks at his mum.*

Agnes   I said – (*parades the dress*) what do you think?

Sol   I dunno.

Agnes   Sister Miriam sewed it for me, as my leaving present.
It doesn't look too similar to the one I wore for Ghana
independence, does it? (*Kisses her teeth.*) Why am I asking you,
you didn't even come. I'm not sure about the hem, though.
I might have to adjust it, so it doesn't drag on the floor. What's
the time?

No response.

Solomon, what is the time?

Sol   I dunno.

Agnes   *Hmm* . . . Uncle Godfrey should be here by now to
pick me up. (*Feeling the dress.*) Hope I don't look too fat. Knowing
Sister Almaz – she'll come with her cooler box full of jellof.
I need to make sure I have extra room for that. (*Laughs.*) What's
the matter with you?

Sol   I dunno, you tell me?

Beat.

Agnes   Would you like to join your mother in celebrating
forty years in this country?

Sol   I'm busy.

Agnes   Busy doing what?

Sol   I'm busy.

Agnes   Well, if you're not coming to church with me tonight
you better be looking for a job. How is it going, anyway?

Sol   Oh, you care now, do you?

Agnes   *Heh!* Is that how you speak to me now?

Sol   I learn from the best.

Agnes (*kisses teeth*)   Miserable, miserable child. Always miserable . . .

Sol   What?

Agnes   I said you are miserable

Sol   I'm waiting for an apology!

Agnes   Apology? Apology for what?

Sol   For the way you spoke to Davina.

Agnes   It is you who should apologise, for pushing your mother.

Sol   I didn't push you.

Agnes   Oh, it was the wind that threw me back, was it?

Sol   Oh, for God's sake . . .

Agnes   *Uh-uh!* No blaspheming in my house!

Sol   All right, all right, I pushed you, I'm sorry, I'm so sorry, okay? Now are you gonna apologise to Davina?

Agnes   Why?

Sol   I think the way you speak to her is out of order!

Agnes   And what about how you speak to me, Solomon? Have you ever checked yourself to see how you treat your mother?

Sol   I haven't done anything / wrong to –

Agnes   When was the last time I ever crossed your mind other than when you wanted something? When was the last time you called home unless you wanted something? When was the last time you visited home without you wanting something?

Sol   I do / think –

Agnes   Even now, the reason why you are here, is it to spend time with your mother and junior brother?

Sol   Yeah / I –

Agnes   No, Solomon! The only reason why you are here is because I am your last resort. You have nowhere else to go. Your girlfriend kicks you out, your friends don't want you, and so you came back here. Is that not the truth, Solomon? Is that not the truth?

Beat.

Sol   I had nowhere else to go / but –

Agnes   Exactly!

Sol   You're my mother, for God's sake!

Agnes   *Uh-uh!* No blaspheming in my house!

Sol   But you are, though! That's what you're suppose to do. You're meant to look after your kids!

Agnes   *Ah . . .* this coming from a person who shouted in my face how he is not a child!

Sol   I didn't shout in your face.

Agnes   But if you are not a child, Solomon, why did you run back to Mummy's house?

Sol   I didn't 'run back to Mummy's house'.

Agnes   Well, what are we to you then? What am I to you? Don't think that you can disregard all I've taught you, live as wild as you want, and then when you find yourself in trouble run back to me. / It doesn't work like that Solomon –

Sol (*sighs*)   I didn't run back to you . . .

Agnes   My patience is drained now. I've finished with you.

Sol   What?

Agnes   I said I'm finished with you!

Sol   What do you mean, you've finished? You can't just wash your hands of me?!

Agnes   Well, you've washed your hands and your brains of all that I've taught you . . .

Sol (*sighs*)   This is ridiculous . . .

Agnes   Next week I leave and I'll be far away. You won't have me to run back to.

Sol   I don't need to run back / to you –

Agnes   You won't have me to tell you what to do.

Sol   I don't need your advice any / more –

Agnes   You will be on your own!

Sol   Good!

Agnes   Just how you want it!

Sol   Just how I want it!

Pause.

Agnes   I only hope Caleb maintains the same level-headedness and sound judgement that I have taught him all these years.

Sol   Here we go. That's it – compare me to Caleb again, the golden child who can do no wrong . . .

Agnes   I'm not comparing. Just stating the facts. He would never disrespect me like this or make stupid decisions.

Sol   Well, it's early days for him *still*. But one day he's gonna make his own choices, some of them you ain't gonna agree on, and just like with me, you're gonna have to deal with it!

Agnes   If he does make foolish decisions it will be because of you and your influence!

Sol   What?

Agnes   If you do not want to listen to me then fine, but don't you dare corrupt his mind!

Sol   Since when did Caleb ever listen to me?

Agnes   As his elder brother, you've had an influence in his growing up!

Sol   There's only been one dominant influence in his life and it ain't me!

He begins to go upstairs. Beat.

Agnes   I remember when you were in primary school and you used to have a little friend called Isabella. Do you remember Isabella? Lovely girl, long curly hair. Of course not, you were too young to remember. You used to call her your girlfriend. I remember your teacher telling me how you used to hold hands every break time. You two could not be separated. Then you met that boy Jerome, *hmm* . . . How he dragged you astray. Poor Isabella, she couldn't understand how you could easily forget about her. (*Beat.*) I still see Isabella's mother in Lewisham market from time to time. She still asks of you and whether you remember Isabella. Last time I saw her mother she told me that Isabella was engaged and was going to move to America with her fiancé. I can't remember what he done, but it was something with lots of money. Such a humble, nice, Catholic girl. She would have been good for you. Very honest and polite . . .

Sol   And how do you know?

Agnes   How do I know what?

Sol   If she's humble, nice, honest and / polite?

Agnes   Because I knew her when she was younger / and I –

Sol   Exactly, when she was younger!

Agnes   Yes, so?

Sol   So what are you judging the girl on? How do you know how she is now?

Agnes   I know these things . . .

Sol   What, cos she had curly hair?

Agnes   Stop being silly.

Sol   Then who's to say she's not a stuck-up, evil, gold-digging bitch?!

Agnes SOLOMON!

Sol But how do you know? Who's to say Jerome didn't save me from heartache, or a life in crime?

Agnes Don't be ridiculous . . .

Sol Life is never gonna be plain sailing, Mum, even if you gave me a manual.

Agnes I didn't say it would be plain sailing. But your road can be much smoother than mine was.

Sol But I need my own experiences to learn from.

Agnes I will not allow my children to walk down the path of destruction.

Sol But at what point do you let your children become adults? At what point do you let go?

Agnes We never let go, Solomon.

Sol But I thought you had finished with me?

Agnes I have. But I'll never let go.

Sol Eh?

Agnes One day when you have kids, in wedlock, you will understand.

Sol But I understand now, Mum. And I fully agree with doing things in 'wedlock' and whatnot. I wanna do things right, set up my family in the right environment. That's what me and Davina hope to achieve together . . .

Agnes Davina?

Sol Yes

Agnes You want to marry Davina?

Sol Yeah, that's always been my plan, you know that?!

Agnes Over my dead body!

Sol I don't believe this . . .

Agnes   Haven't you listen to anything I've said?

Sol   Haven't you listen to anything I've said?

Agnes   Listen to me now. I named you after King Solomon, because of his great wisdom. I hope one day you live up to that name and realise that girl is no good for / you!

Sol   Here we go again, same old speech . . .

Agnes   She's not serious. She'll give you two years of marriage max, then she'll be gone!

Sol   Why are you threaten by her?

Agnes   I'm not threaten by that girl.

Sol   Does she remind you of yourself at her age or something?

Agnes   What is this nonsense you are saying now?

Sol   Or are you just plain jealous?

Agnes   Now you listen to me, / you are –

Sol   What? What are you gonna do, slap me? You make me laugh –

Agnes   If you want to follow her off a cliff, that's fine by me.

Sol   Well, I'd rather learn from my own mistakes than follow in your shoes. I'll only end up old and lonely, with two kids from different partners!

Agnes   What?

Sol   You came to this country all them years ago, on your own, away from your mummy and daddy, thinking you had it sussed. But within a few years you ended up on your own, having to raise not one but two kids, from two different men / which –

Agnes *slaps* **Sol** *across the face. Pause.*

Sol   Truth hurts, *innit*?

Agnes   I want you out of my house.

Beat.

Sol   Okay.

He exits.

Scene Ten

Night time. **Mehmet** *comes into the living room via the front door, which is open. He begins to pick up bits of clothing and other items around the sofa.* **Sol** *enters.*

Mehmet   Why are there bits of your clothes randomly scattered around the living room?

Sol   I was in a rush, *innit?* Just been flinging stuff on the sofa as I find them.

Mehmet (*holds up a pair of boxer shorts with his finger tips*)   Are these yours or your mum's?

Sol   Ha ha.

Mehmet   Are these clean or dirty?

Sol *snatches the boxer shorts off* **Mehmet**.

Sol   Give me them! (*He smells them, then puts them into his bag.*) And yes, they are clean.

Mehmet (*crouching to look under the sofa*)   You're gonna have to move this you know?! I think you got some socks and that underneath.

Sol   Come off my mum's carpet!

Mehmet   What?

Sol   Take off your shoes if you're gonna stand there.

Mehmet *sighs as he takes off his shoes and throws them at the door.*

Sol   Watch the door!

Mehmet   All right, *man.* Damn, so many rules in this house.

Sol   Well, you better get used to it, cos I'm gonna ban all footwear in my flat as well.

Mehmet   Why?

Sol   It makes sense, *innit*, keeps the place tidier.

Mehmet   Davina must be pleased.

Sol   Yep. Cos it means less hoovering for her.

Mehmet *and* **Sol** *laugh.*

Mehmet   Here ya!

Finds a sock and throws it at **Sol**. *It hits his mouth.*

Sol   Urgh! It's got a cobweb on it!

Mehmet   Good. Let the taste be a reminder that you owe me money!

Sol   Yeah, you'll get it back, I promise.

Mehmet   I told my uncle that I needed to borrow money to fix my car. He might get suspicious if he catches me doing all these journeys.

Sol   Don't worry, I'll get it back to you a-sap. All I needed was some emergency funds. Davina weren't gonna let that subject go. You know how it is – 'no romance without finance'.

Mehmet   'You gotta have a J.O.B. if you wanna be with me.'

Sol *looks at* **Mehmet**.

Mehmet   I'm quoting the song, *innit* (*Sings.*) 'Ain't nothing going on but the rent'?

Sol   Oh, *seen* . . . Thought you was getting funny on me . . .

Mehmet   You wish!

Sol   About to remind a man that I got a woman . . .

Mehmet   All right 'King Solomon'.

The two laugh. **Mehmet** *runs his hands under the sofa.*

Mehmet   I think that's all the stuff from under there.

Sol   Okay. Make sure you push the chair back to exactly the same spot or my mum will make up noise.

Mehmet   What?

Sol (*laughs*)   I'm joking. Just make sure it's straight.

The lights come on in the living room. **Caleb** *is at the foot of the stairs in his night wear – boxers and Thundercats T-shirt.*

Caleb   What's going on?

Sol   What you doing up?

Caleb   I wanted to get a glass of milk, I couldn't sleep. What you up to?

Sol   I'm going.

Caleb   Going where?

Sol   Home to my woman.

Caleb   Oh.

Beat.

Sol   Don't look too surprise, Caleb. You won. From next week the house will be all yours.

Mehmet   *Innit*, cheer up, *man*! You gonna have your very own bachelor pad here.

Sol   It might get a bit lonely being in a three-bedroom house all on your own. So I promise one day soon, I'll teach you the art of courting . . . a.k.a. '*drawing gyal*' .

Mehmet *and* **Sol** *laugh.*

Caleb   Does Mum know you're moving back with Davina?

Sol   What?

Caleb   I said, does Mum know you're moving back in with Davina?

Sol   Nope.

Caleb   Are you gonna tell her?

Sol   Nope.

Caleb   Don't you think you should tell her?

Sol   Yeah, well . . .

Caleb   So, aren't you gonna?

Sol   It doesn't concern you.

Beat.

Caleb   Typical Sol . . .

He goes into the kitchen. Beat.

Mehmet   It's a shame you two can't patch things up before she goes away.

Sol   Me and Caleb will be at war until one of us dies . . .

Mehmet   I'm talking about your mum.

Sol   Oh. Well . . . I tried . . . but she didn't wanna know and I guess I've got to accept that's how it'll always be. (*Beat.*) You don't think she's bad, do you?

Mehmet   Which one?

Sol   Davina.

Mehmet   I don't think your girlfriend or your mum are bad. They both love you, and love makes people do some crazy things, even makes them jealous of other people who love you.

Sol   But I've known you for ten years and you haven't got a problem with Davina.

Mehmet   But I never said I loved you.

Sol   You know what I mean.

Mehmet   But it's different between me and Davina anyway. She's female, I like females and, most importantly, I know how to talk to females.

Sol   What do you mean, you know how to talk to females?

Mehmet   I know how to get along with them, tell them what they want to hear and that.

Sol   And what have you been telling Davina to help you two 'get along'?

Mehmet (*laughs*)   You're so paranoid, *man*, relax!

Caleb *comes out of the kitchen with a glass of milk in hand.*

Caleb   Well . . . I guess this is *sayonara* . . . for the mean time.

Sol   Yeah, you just make sure you don't destroy Mum's house.

Caleb   And how or why would I do that?

Mehmet   Parties? Girls?

Sol (*to* **Mehmet**)   See, I was thinking to say that, but then I remembered, he hasn't got any friends.

Mehmet   Oh, *seen* . . .

Caleb   Just make sure you don't slam the door when you leave. (*Goes to the stairs.*) Oh yeah, and I will be changing the locks next week, so you'll need to call ahead if you wish to visit. *Au revoir.*

He exits upstairs. **Sol** *kisses his teeth.* **Mehmet** *collects the last few things. Beat.*

Sol   It's not a nice feeling, you know?

Mehmet   What's not?

Sol   Women fighting over you . . . these women, anyway. I mean, how can I choose between the woman that gave me life and the woman I wanna spend my life with? This is crazy.

Mehmet   I gotta admit, I wouldn't like to be in your position. But you gotta do 'you'. You can't live your life for other people.

Sol   Yeah, I know.

Mehmet   And people's opinions can swing either way over time.

Sol   True, but with my mum I know in the back of her mind she will always think that I could of done better.

Mehmet   Only you know how you truly feel about being with Davina, so only you can say whether you've struck gold or you are settling for second best.

Sol   True.

Beat.

Sol   But you know . . . parents have a way of being right about certain things . . . sometimes.

Mehmet   Well . . . you better hope she's wrong this time round.

Beat.

Sol   I do love my mum, you know?

Mehmet   I didn't say you didn't . . .

Sol   Just in case. Cos all you been hearing is me cussing her.

Mehmet   Well, as long as you know that, that's all that matters. Cos I tell you now, bro, she always will. Mothers never let go, *man*.

Sol   That's scary, *boi*, she said the same thing.

Mehmet   *Rar*, is it?

Sol   Yeah, *man*. Imma call you Yoda from now on.

The two laugh.

All right, enough of this chat now. Man and man ain't meant to be talking like this.

Mehmet   I'm used to it, *boi*. Everyone always comes to me for advice.

Sol   Is it? Well, forget Yoda then, I should call you Trisha!

They pick up the last things and begin to head to the exit.

Mehmet   *Allow* it, *man*.

Sol   All right . . . Jeremy Kyle. (*Laughs.*)

Mehmet   And a 'Hell no!' to that as well!

Sol *laughs.* **Agnes** *calls from upstairs.*

Agnes   *Solomon?* (*Beat.*) Solomon?

For a moment **Sol** *stops and ponders whether to reply.* **Agnes**'s *footsteps are heard coming down the stairs.* **Sol** *hurries to the door and exits.* **Agnes** *comes to the foot of the stairs.*

Agnes   Solomon?

She looks around but no one is to be found.

Scene Eleven

The final day before **Agnes**'s *departure, mid-afternoon. In the living room* **Agnes** *is packing a bag.* **Caleb** *comes down the stairs carrying a suitcase.*

Caleb   Are you sure you'll be able to carry this?

Agnes   What am I carrying? I'll just be pulling.

Caleb   Yeah, but what about when you have to take it off the conveyer belt?

Agnes   I'll be fine.

Caleb   What about when you reach your new Ghanaian palace? In the picture, I'm sure I saw lots of stairs.

Agnes   I'll be fine.

Caleb   Are you sure, Mum? If there's anything in here you don't need I can send it over to you / next week . . .

Agnes   I'll be fine. And for the last time, take off your shoes if you are going to walk on the carpet!

Caleb   Sorry.

He carefully walks around the edges of the rug.

Agnes Now, I've left this place in a healthy condition. It's now up to you to maintain it. So don't get any funny ideas to leave your job to become a musician or anything.

Caleb Don't worry, I've seen the adverts. 'My home is at risk if I don't keep up with my repayments.' (*Laughs.*)

Agnes They are not joking, so make sure you do. Make sure you cut down your credit card usage as well.

Caleb Yeah, I know.

Agnes You need to make sure you have the least amount of outgoings each month as possible.

Caleb Yeah, I know.

Agnes Remember the gas and electricity is quarterly, so you need to make sure you make allowances for that.

Caleb I've already turned it into a monthly direct debit thingy.

Agnes And if you want to continue using the internet . . .

Caleb Mother dear, it's all right – I've got it all under control.

Agnes This isn't like paying mobile phone bills, you know?

Caleb I know.

Agnes And you'll have no one else to help you but yourself.

Caleb I know.

Agnes And try not to take out any more loans . . .

Caleb I won't, Mum . . .

Agnes That will drain your money further.

Caleb I know.

Agnes Have you finished paying your student loan?

Caleb I wish.

Agnes   Well, that is another thing you need to take into consideration.

Caleb   And I will, Mum, I've got it all planned out. Everything is gonna be all right.

Agnes   *Hmm . . .*

Caleb   Trust me.

Agnes   Just don't lose your brain. Remember all that I've taught you.

Caleb   Of course I will, how can I ever forget?

He struggles to close a suitcase.

This ain't gonna shut, Mum.

Agnes (*laughs*)   You've still got much to learn.

She takes over from **Caleb**.

Agnes   When I first came to this country, I managed to pack twice as much things into one suitcase that was half the size of this one.

Caleb   Yeah, yeah . . .

Agnes   It's true. If you just persevere you will always find extra room.

She closes the suitcase.

See what happens when you don't give up.

Caleb   All right, all right.

Beat.

Agnes   So, how is work going?

Caleb   It's all good. I think I might go back into the office tomorrow, need to arrange some meetings with a few clients. Problem with working at home is that you can't keep an eye on the troops, which is essential, if you want excellent productivity.

Agnes   *Ah ah*, my son the big shot! (*Laughs.*) You know, in forty years I've worked in so many places, I can't even remember all of them. I've worked in biscuit factories, schools, hospitals, even in television.

Caleb   Serious? You worked in television?

Agnes   Yes. One of my first jobs was at the BBC, working in the staff canteen.

Caleb   Oh.

Agnes   Yes, I've ran the good race and I've fought the good fight. And now you get to reap the benefits, so cheer up – (*handing* **Caleb** *a bag*) and take this to the door.

Caleb   I thought your flight's at ten?

Agnes   You get to the airport at least four hours early, just in case.

Caleb   In case what? The flight being called early or something? I think that's highly unlikely.

Agnes   In case of eventualities. Listen to me: I've flown many times before, so I know what I'm talking about, okay?

Caleb   Okay, just sounds a bit early. But you're the boss, I guess . . . for the mean time.

Agnes   Even when I am gone I will still be the boss, and don't you forget it.

Beat.

Caleb   I don't know what I'm gonna do on Sunday.

Agnes   What do you mean?

Caleb   Without your cooking!

Agnes (*laughs*)   You know how to cook.

Caleb   Yeah, but it ain't the same.

Agnes   Just cook oven chips, nice and simple.

Caleb   But even that wouldn't be the same as you doing it. You put that mothering touch in it that makes it extra special.

Agnes   Every child says that about their mother's cooking.

Caleb   Well, I don't know about every child's mother, but I know about mine and I think she's the best.

Agnes   Well . . . I do try.

Caleb   Don't be embarrassed to take the credit.

Agnes   I'm not. (*Beat.*) Thank you, Caleb. You were always one to show your appreciation.

Caleb   I'm sure Sol is grateful too . . . in his own strange way.

Agnes   If he doesn't miss me while I'm in the country, what makes you think he'll miss me when I'm gone?

Beat.

Caleb   Well . . . I'll miss you.

Agnes   And that's why you'll always be my little boy. (*Beat.*) Come here.

Caleb   Why?

Agnes   Just come.

Caleb *walks over.*

Agnes   Not on the carpet!

Caleb (*sighs*)   You asked me to come!

Agnes *sighs. She walks to* **Caleb** *and gives him a hug.*

Agnes   I'm proud of you and all that you have achieved. You have a bright future ahead of you – don't let no man or woman rob it from you, you hear me?

Caleb   I won't.

Agnes   Don't let the evil influences in this world corrupt you either. Never change.

Caleb   Okay.

Agnes (*looks at her watch*)   Where is your Uncle Godfrey? Time is ticking.

Beat.

Caleb   Mum?

Agnes   *Hmm?* (*Beat.*) What?

Caleb   It's nothing, but . . . well . . .

Agnes   What?

Caleb   What would make you most proud of me, while you were gone?

Agnes   That you pay your bills on time and don't lose the house.

Caleb   Other than that.

Agnes   That you stay debt free.

Caleb   Other than the financial stuff.

Agnes   Well . . . that you continue to be successful . . . and you continue to make the right decisions in life, like I've taught you.

Caleb   What about in terms of family? And starting my own . . . ?

Agnes   Of course I want to be a grandmother, I'm not getting any younger! But you need a wife for that.

Caleb   Yeah.

Agnes   Why? Have you found someone?

Caleb *smiles.*

Agnes   *Eh?* Caleb? You've found someone?

Caleb   Well . . . / not –

Agnes   Tell me. This isn't the time to get shy.

The door is heard unlocking. **Sol** *enters into the room, hand in hand with* **Davina**.

Caleb (*sighs*)   Just as I was getting use to life as an only child.

Sol   Mum? We just wanted to come by and wish you all the best and . . . that we will miss you.

Agnes (*points at* **Davina**)   Including her? Don't make me laugh . . .

Sol   I'm not here to argue, Mum, I'm just here to say goodbye in a civil manner, like adults.

Agnes   Oh yes, of course, because you are a man now, so your word is final.

Sol (*to* **Davina**)   I tried.

Agnes   So this wasn't your idea?

Sol   What?

Agnes   You needed her to tell you what to do?

Sol   No!

Agnes   Now you can't even think for yourself.

Sol   You're amazing – even now you still wanna fight.

Agnes   This is not about fighting; it's about your stubbornness!

Sol   All I wanted to do was wish you well! (*Sighs. To* **Caleb**.) Here. (*Throws* **Caleb** *his house keys.*) I won't be needing them any more. (*To* **Davina**.) Come on.

Sol *goes to exit.*

Caleb   *Auf wiedersehen!*

Davina (*to* **Sol**)   No, not yet. (*To* **Agnes**.) Look, I really don't understand what Sol has done wrong?! I know myself, and I ain't a bad person . . .

Agnes *kisses her teeth.*

Davina   Okay, I threw him out. But I was stressed . . .

Agnes   Stressed? *Ha!*

Davina   Yes. Stressed because of what you put me through! I've never been spoken to like the way you speak to me. I don't

know why you think I'm out to destroy your son. How can
I destroy someone I love more than myself?

Agnes *kisses her teeth.*

Davina   You know I actually told him to go back to you, cos
from the way you were acting you obviously needed him more
than I did. But you know what? I ain't gonna give up just like
that . . . He may be your son, but he's also my boyfriend. And
I can't live my life without him.

Caleb   So, would you say he's your 'Sol mate'?

Agnes / Sol   *Shut up!*

Caleb   I thought it was funny.

Agnes *kisses her teeth towards* **Caleb**. *He goes into the kitchen.*

Davina   Look, basically I just wanted to tell you that even
though you don't like me . . . I'm gonna respect you, cos you're
the mother of my man. If it wasn't for you, he wouldn't be
here and . . . I wouldn't be happy . . . and that's it.

Beat.

Agnes (*sighs*)   You're not right for him, my dear, it's not your
fault. It's just not meant to be. Maybe when you grow up and
have children of your own, you'll understand, okay?

Sol *sighs. There's a knock at the door.*

Agnes   Who is it?

Michaela *enters into the living room.*

Michaela   Oh . . . hi.

Agnes   Hello.

Michaela   . . . Hi.

Beat

Agnes   Can I help you?

Caleb *re-enters the living room with a glass of milk.*

Michaela   Sorry, I didn't know you were still . . .

Caleb   It's all right, Mum, she came to see me. I'll be back in a minute.

He goes to the door.

Michaela   It's all right, Caleb, I'm not stopping.

Caleb   Why didn't you call first?

Michaela   I've been trying to get hold of you all week!

Caleb   Must be something wrong with my phone.

Michaela   Yeah, right. Listen, you're not going to get paid for your unauthorised absence. / Stuart's –

Caleb   It wasn't technically an unauthorised absence.

Michaela   Well, whatever you want to call it, Stuart's not happy with you not showing up for work and has asked me to start looking for a replacement.

Caleb   You serious?

Agnes   But for the past week he's been working from home.

Michaela   Really? I didn't know you could sort out the office mail from your bedroom, Caleb?

Agnes   Office mail?

Michaela   Look, if you're not willing to work things out between us then we got to be civil. I mean . . . you're a bright kid. It would be silly to lose your first job because of me.

Agnes   Who are you?

Michaela   Sorry, Agnes, I honestly thought . . . (*Sighs.*) Sorry, I didn't want to meet you this way.

Michaela *hurries to the exit.*

Agnes   How do you know my name?

Michaela *exits.*

Agnes   Caleb, who is she? (*Beat.*) Caleb?

Caleb   She's just . . . a work colleague.

Agnes   A work colleague?

Sol (*to* **Caleb**)   So all this time you been working in a mailroom?

Davina *nudges him in the ribs.*

Davina (*to* **Sol**)   Stop it!

Agnes   Caleb, I'm going to ask you again, who was that woman? (*Beat.*) I'm waiting. (*Beat.*) Well?

Sol   It's all right, Mum, I'll talk to him. You got to get / going . . .

Agnes   Caleb Moses Kwajo Mensah, your mother asked you a question!

Caleb   Yes, and I heard it! (*Sighs.*) She's just . . . a friend . . .

Agnes   A friend?

Caleb   An ex-friend.

Agnes   A girlfriend?

Caleb   Ex-girlfriend!

Agnes   What? That big woman?

Caleb   Before you start, I know what you're going to say . . .

Agnes   Oh, you do?

Sol   Mum, let's not do this / now –

Agnes   Caleb, start talking.

Beat.

Sol   Mum . . .

Agnes   Caleb, start talking. I want to know what you've been up to. (*Beat.*) Caleb?

Caleb   Yes! We went out, okay? And . . . and . . . I really did like her.

Agnes   What else?

Caleb   There's nothing else . . .

Agnes   So why were you hiding from her?

Caleb   I wasn't hiding from her . . .

Agnes   Then why were you hiding her from me? (*Beat.*) I asked you a question!

Sol   Mum, please . . .

Agnes (*to* **Sol**)   Did you know about this?

Sol   No –

Agnes   I warned you about your influence –

Sol   I didn't know –

Agnes   I told you not to corrupt him. See what has happened / now –

Caleb   Mum, Sol had nothing to do with it. I was just . . . just . . .

Agnes   Just what?

Caleb   Just . . . protecting her.

Agnes   Protecting her from what?

Caleb   Protecting her . . . from you . . . But it doesn't matter now.

Agnes   How long have you been lying to me about this . . . this . . . woman?

Caleb   It doesn't matter now . . .

Agnes   Before I leave this house, you will tell me!

Caleb   It doesn't matter now.

Agnes   Tell me!

Caleb (*sighs*)   I'm fed up. I can't do this any more . . . I just want to live my life, without all of this.

Agnes   What do you mean?

Caleb   Why should I of allowed Michaela to go through what Davina went through? No one deserves that, but do you care?

Sol   All right, Caleb . . .

Caleb   No, you don't! But this is my life, Mum; you can shout as much as you want but you can't stop me from living my life!

Agnes   I never –

Caleb   And if it means you don't trust me with the house any more then . . . then . . . fair enough.

Pause.

Sol   Caleb –

Davina (*to* **Sol**)   Don't –

Pause. **Agnes** *sighs.*

Agnes   Caleb . . . Caleb, come here.

Caleb   I don't want to argue, Mum . . .

Agnes   Come.

Caleb *walks over to* **Agnes**.

Agnes (*sighs*)   Caleb, Caleb, Caleb.

She smiles at **Caleb** *and hugs him.*

Agnes   Solomon?

Sol   Yes, Mum?

Agnes   Come.

Sol *walks over to* **Agnes**. *She gives him a hug.*

Agnes   Look at my handsome boys. So . . . so . . . handsome. (*Beat.*) Know your mother loves you very . . . very much.

Sol   We know you do, Mum. (*To* **Caleb**.) Don't we?

Caleb   . . . Yeah . . . yeah.

Agnes   Good.

Agnes *goes to her suitcase and sighs.*

Davina (*to* **Sol**)   I told you things would work out.

Sol   All right . . .

Davina   Would you like me to help you with your stuff, Mrs Mensah?

Agnes   No, thank you. (*Beat.*) Caleb . . . Take my suitcase upstairs. Make sure you don't step on my beautiful, beautiful carpet.

Sol   What time's your flight, Mum?

Caleb   Yeah, I thought you said you were going to the airport early?

Agnes   Yes . . . but my work here is not yet complete.

Sol   What do you mean?

Agnes   When you are a parent, your life is no more your own. One day, when you two are older, you will understand.

Caleb   Okay, but what's that got to do with getting to the airport?

Agnes   If you boys don't listen to me, then you will never become men. So until you do . . . I will be staying right here.

Davina   Oh God, no . . .

Agnes   Solomon, see your blasphemous friend out, please.

Agnes *goes to the sofa and sits down.*

Davina   Sol?

Sol   Mum?

Agnes   I asked nicely didn't I? I didn't shout or raise my voice . . .

Caleb   Mum, you can't give up your plans like that? You've been looking forward to this for long time. Mum, are you listening? You got to get to the airport. (*He carries the suitcase to the front door.*) Come on Mum, let's go. Mum? Come on, let's go. Mum? Mum? Mum?

Methuen Drama Student Editions

Methuen Drama Modern Plays

include work by

Edward Albee
Jean Anouilh
John Arden
Margaretta D'Arcy
Peter Barnes
Sebastian Barry
Brendan Behan
Dermot Bolger
Edward Bond
Bertolt Brecht
Howard Brenton
Anthony Burgess
Simon Burke
Jim Cartwright
Caryl Churchill
Noël Coward
Lucinda Coxon
Sarah Daniels
Nick Darke
Nick Dear
Shelagh Delaney
David Edgar
David Eldridge
Dario Fo
Michael Frayn
John Godber
Paul Godfrey
David Greig
John Guare
Peter Handke
David Harrower
Jonathan Harvey
Iain Heggie
Declan Hughes
Terry Johnson
Sarah Kane
Charlotte Keatley
Barrie Keeffe
Howard Korder

Robert Lepage
Doug Lucie
Martin McDonagh
John McGrath
Terrence McNally
David Mamet
Patrick Marber
Arthur Miller
Mtwa, Ngema & Simon
Tom Murphy
Phyllis Nagy
Peter Nichols
Sean O'Brien
Joseph O'Connor
Joe Orton
Louise Page
Joe Penhall
Luigi Pirandello
Stephen Poliakoff
Franca Rame
Mark Ravenhill
Philip Ridley
Reginald Rose
Willy Russell
Jean-Paul Sartre
Sam Shepard
Wole Soyinka
Simon Stephens
Shelagh Stephenson
Peter Straughan
C. P. Taylor
Theatre de Complicite
Theatre Workshop
Sue Townsend
Judy Upton
Timberlake Wertenbaker
Roy Williams
Snoo Wilson
Victoria Wood

Methuen Drama Contemporary Dramatists

include

John Arden (two volumes)
Arden & D'Arcy
Peter Barnes (three volumes)
Sebastian Barry
Dermot Bolger
Edward Bond (eight volumes)
Howard Brenton
    (two volumes)
Richard Cameron
Jim Cartwright
Caryl Churchill
    (two volumes)
Sarah Daniels (two volumes)
Nick Darke
David Edgar (three volumes)
David Eldridge
Ben Elton
Dario Fo (two volumes)
Michael Frayn (three volumes)
John Godber (three volumes)
Paul Godfrey
David Greig
John Guare
Lee Hall (two volumes)
Peter Handke
Jonathan Harvey
    (two volumes)
Declan Hughes
Terry Johnson (three volumes)
Sarah Kane
Barrie Keeffe
Bernard-Marie Koltès
    (two volumes)
David Lan
Bryony Lavery
Deborah Levy
Doug Lucie

David Mamet (four volumes)
Martin McDonagh
Duncan McLean
Anthony Minghella
    (two volumes)
Tom Murphy (five volumes)
Phyllis Nagy
Anthony Neilson
Philip Osment
Gary Owen
Louise Page
Stewart Parker (two volumes)
Joe Penhall
Stephen Poliakoff
    (three volumes)
David Rabe
Mark Ravenhill
Christina Reid
Philip Ridley
Willy Russell
Eric-Emmanuel Schmitt
Ntozake Shange
Sam Shepard (two volumes)
Wole Soyinka (two volumes)
Simon Stephens
Shelagh Stephenson
David Storey (three volumes)
Sue Townsend
Judy Upton
Michel Vinaver
    (two volumes)
Arnold Wesker (two volumes)
Michael Wilcox
Roy Williams (two volumes)
Snoo Wilson (two volumes)
David Wood (two volumes)
Victoria Wood

Methuen Drama World Classics

include

Jean Anouilh (two volumes)
Brendan Behan
Aphra Behn
Bertolt Brecht (eight volumes)
Büchner
Bulgakov
Calderón
Čapek
Anton Chekhov
Noël Coward (eight volumes)
Feydeau
Eduardo De Filippo
Max Frisch
John Galsworthy
Gogol
Gorky (two volumes)
Harley Granville Barker
  (two volumes)
Victor Hugo
Henrik Ibsen (six volumes)
Jarry

Lorca (three volumes)
Marivaux
Mustapha Matura
David Mercer (two volumes)
Arthur Miller (five volumes)
Molière
Musset
Peter Nichols (two volumes)
Joe Orton
A. W. Pinero
Luigi Pirandello
Terence Rattigan
  (two volumes)
W. Somerset Maugham
  (two volumes)
August Strindberg
  (three volumes)
J. M. Synge
Ramón del Valle-Inclan
Frank Wedekind
Oscar Wilde